Why Can't You Just Eat?: A Look Inside the Mind of Anorexia, Bulimia, and Binge Eating Disorder
Copyright © 2015 by Shannon Lagasse

The content of this book is for general instruction only. Each person's physical, emotional, and spiritual condition is unique. The instruction in this book is not intended to replace or interrupt the reader's relationship with a physician or other professional. Please consult your doctor for matters pertaining to your specific health and diet.

To contact the author, visit www.HungerforHappiness.com.

Printed in the United States of America.

ISBN 10: 1508850852
ISBN 13: 978-1508850854

D0834787

Dedication

This book is for all the girls and boys, men and women, out there who are struggling with an eating disorder and feel lost, confused, and misunderstood.

It is for the moms and dads who want their kids to get better, whose mantra remains, "Why can't you just eat?"

This is for the friends and family members, teachers and onlookers, who notice the signs of an eating disorder, but are woefully unsure of what to do in this kind of situation. How can they best support someone? How can you break the ice on a topic that is not only taboo, but intensely personal and riddled with back stories?

Why Can't You Just Eat? is for all those people like me who just want (or wanted) someone to understand – not change or convince or coerce, but just GET what's going on.

If you're reading this, this one's for you. May you finally feel heard and understood, or may you finally understand what it is like to recover from ED (eating disorder).

Intention

We all have a story to tell. And every story ever told, like every painting ever painted, is colored by our own lenses, by the perspective through which we see the world. So, while this story is entirely truthful, please keep in mind that this tale was woven based on my own version of my life experience, which may not sound like any other version of this story from any other character who was present at the time.

No family is without secrets or drama. In pulling back the curtains on ED, I am also pulling back the curtains on my home life, on what happened behind closed doors or when others were not around. Please know that I do not judge my family or myself for our actions. I truly believe we are all doing the best we can do with the beliefs we have at the time and that who we were is not reflective of who we each, individually and collectively, are today.

Eating disorders are as varied as they are complex. They're not the easiest illnesses to understand, but they aresome of the deadliest, which is why the writing of this book has been calling to me. I want to finally pull back the curtains and bring you behind the scenes of what it's like to struggle with anorexia, bulimia, binge eating disorder, depression, body dysmorphia, and emotional eating.

The tone of this book is much like that of a thriller. The way I tell the story brings you along for the ride as you read about the mindset and the behaviors that accompany an eating disorder.

There are so many misconceptions around what eating disorders are, how they form, how to treat them, and how to work with patients with ED. My deepest hope is that this book will help to clear up some of those gray areas so that those who are struggling can get the support they so desperately need to survive.

Introduction

About 5 years ago, I was dying.

Slowly but surely, I was starving my body of nutrients, depleting my bones and muscle mass, and sacrificing memories and brain function for the chance to be thin.

Not that I thought being thin was going to solve all of my problems, but it gave me something to focus on other than what was going on in my life. It took my attention away from issues that seemed unsolvable, tension that seemed thick enough to choke the living daylights out of me, and the verbal abuse I suffered regularly that made the bullying I received from classmates seem normal and to be expected, as if I were deserving of such harsh and critical words.

You see, there's a misconception in the world of eating disorders that one develops anorexia out of the desire to be thin, that vanity rules the mind and drives us to starve ourselves to an ideal yet unattainable look of perfection.

But that's just not true.

When the desire to be thin is present, it's covering up something else. An eating disorder, like any compulsion, is a coping mechanism, a way of avoiding a deeper issue that one is struggling with. It's a plea, a cry for help, when no words would do our wounds justice or when we feel our voice would be just a cry to the wind – lost and unreturned. Just like a cutter may slice into their skin to unleash physical pain that doesn't come close to matching the intensity of their internal struggle, anorexics and bulimics use food to express that which they dare not speak about, that which they are scared to give voice to, because then it makes their problems REAL. The desire to be thin, I've found, is often a desire to hide. But what are we hiding from?

That's the real question, and one that isn't asked often enough.

In my recovery, I've found that, more often than not, people would tell me why I had an eating disorder. They asked no questions and made only assumptions. Their expertise, it seemed, qualified them to be an expert on my life and on my experience.

Interesting.

The thing is, only the person suffering knows what's really going on. The best the rest of us can do is guess.

And there are lots of things that come up time and again with regard to what is going on in the mind of someone with an eating disorder.

There are so, so many reasons why one might engage in these behaviors (and the above is by no means an exhaustive list), so why do we automatically assume that they are done out of a desire for vanity or attention?

I believe this is due to not only a lack of awareness, but misinformation that is spread by the media. It is so much easier to blame the individual, saying, "He's just doing it to get attention" or "She's just being vain" like this is some Miley Cyrus shenanigan than it is to acknowledge that, in the society we live in, a lot of us are fucked up. We are not raised with the capability nor the opportunity to authentically express ourselves. We are taught from a young age not to trust the wisdom of our body and spirit. We allow our media to alter images of men and women to an unattainable and often unhealthy ideal, and we think that this is OK. After all, it's what everyone else is doing. It's what everyone else is reading and buying into. So why shouldn't we?

Now, maybe this is an over-generalization here, but when we look at the number of compulsions and addictions out there – ranging from the mild eyeballs-glued-to-the-TV-for-4-hours-a-night to the more severe I'm-strung-out-on-heroin-and-ready-to-kill-for-my-next-fix – it's easy to see that we're missing the forest for the trees. This isn't a problem that is solely related to nutrition or better parenting or media legislature; this is a problem with the way we have collectively agreed to live our lives. As a society, we have swept our imperfections under a rug and painted our faces with masks of fake bliss. But what happens when we do this is that we find ourselves alone, drowning in a sea of perceived perfection, when really, underneath the surface, we are all gasping for air.

It is time to allow our finish to be tarnished, to be brave enough and vulnerable enough to allow our cracks to show, because we all have them. We live in a world where problems are kept in closets or behind closed doors, and it is considered shameful to "air your dirty laundry". But, truth be told, we all have enough dirty laundry to fill up a laundromat 12 times over. Our entire lives, we have been keeping the whole show under wraps. We have been stifling the voice that yearned to cry out for help when we needed it most. We have avoided our pain, numbed it and tranquilized it, in any number of ways. And if we are willing to look at our own methods of avoidance, we are able to at least glimpse into the mindset of an eating disorder, as this is avoidance taken to a whole new self-destructive measure. ("It is better to be hurting than to feel this").

In this book, you will read stories of my experiences with anorexia, bulimia, and binge eating disorder. I have attempted to flesh out and fill in enough of the story for you to be able to feel like you are there with me to give you an idea of what the internal struggle is like. You will hear the voices that echoed in my head for years, the ones that told me I was not good enough or that I needed to try harder, to be someone else, in order to be loved. You might even relate to some of these messages. You will take a journey from a period of deprivation and starvation, skin and bones, to a time of such extreme excess that every night ended in a bloated, swollen tummy and endless shame. And my hope is that through the understanding you gain on multiple facets of having an eating disorder, you will be fearless in your recovery, your support of a loved one, or your advocacy for eating disorder awareness.

Fall 2008 – The Start of My Eating Disorder

My daddy left me when I was 14 years old. And when I say "me", I mean "us" – my sister and I. He left *us* to face a pile of boxes full of our belongings on my mother's front porch with no hello and no forewarning, not even the chance to say goodbye to my former home. I didn't really know how I felt about it then. It seemed like I didn't really know WHAT to think, let alone how to feel.

When we kept asking why, what we'd done to deserve this exile from our home of 6 years, my father brought us to the beach and sat us each down with a 17-page letter outlining the past 8 years of what life had been like since he and my mother divorced.

In that letter, he divulged all the dirty details of what had transpired between himself, my mother, and my stepmom (whom we called "Steppy") over the course of several years. All of the transgressions he had kept secret, all the frustrating and time-consuming back and forths he'd held back in an effort to maintain neutrality between households. All of this was to comply with what the books considered "healthy parenting after divorce," where neither parent speaks ill of the other.

With all of this laid out in front of us, it made more sense as to why he'd want to put a simple end to the neverending custody battles that he'd been waging in court with my mother since their divorce in 1998.

Coupled with the fact that we had openly disliked my stepmom (thanks in large part to my mother's constant trash talking of her character), as well as our childish desire to escape discipline and consequence in favor of my mother's care, where rules and responsibility went out the window, it was no wonder my father would want to keep us away from his fiancée.

But that didn't change the fact that, to my 14-year-old mind, my father was choosing his partner over his children.

Over the years, I had slowly been losing my dad as a parental figure, as much of the authority was handed over to Steppy, to whom discipline came quite naturally, often in the form of lengthy lectures, writing lines over and over again on lined paper, and what I've now come to recognize, with the help of lots of therapy, as abuse: nails dug into the arms as we were pushed into walls, being pushed down the stairs, being yelled at and called names.

And, now, with this move, I had lost my father almost entirely.

To some, it would not seem so bad. I mean, it's not like he wasn't around at all anymore. It's not like he left when I was born. He wasn't some deadbeat who couldn't bear to raise children. He wasn't some irresponsible jackass who would leave his baby mama hanging. No, my dad was an ordinary man who simply chose the love of his life over his own flesh and blood. And, somehow, that made it that much more difficult to deal with.

In the months that followed, I spent hours locked in my room, lying on the floor crying to Josh Groban's album "Awake". To this day, I cannot listen to the song "You Are Loved" without it bringing tears to my eyes. I pitied myself. *You poor thing*, I thought, *Your dad leaving you behind so he can be with his fiancée. What did you ever do to deserve this? You've been such a good girl.*

Ahhh… the good girl. It's amazing how often we think that by playing the part of the "good girl", we'll get exactly what we want. Too bad it never works out that way.

A year after that fateful day in August when we were kicked out of our home, I started my first diet. I still could not tell you what the impetus was for this decision, although I know I could not sum it up with just one word or phrase or experience. It wasn't one THING that made me want to be better or thinner; it was the accumulation of many such things.

It started off innocently enough: I simply started walking everywhere. The mile and a half to work at the florist. The 2 miles to work out at my gym. 8 miles to the library. When I was walking, I felt the weight of the world fall off my shoulders. I felt like I was one with everything. It was during one of these early walks that I had my first experience of enlightenment, connection to everything, that knowing that everything was perfect exactly as it was, that I was safe, provided for, and taken care of.

Then I started to change my diet. I had already been vegetarian, but now I started to cut back on other foods that I was eating. I adopted a vegan lifestyle, removing dairy and eggs from my diet. I stopped consuming oil and salt, preferring Mrs. Dash, which, according to the magazines I was reading, would flavor anything and not contribute to bloat. I cut back on my portions, telling myself that I wasn't growing anymore, only outwards. A girl of my age did not need to be eating nearly as much as I was.

In my head, I heard the voices of my family. My Grampy, who would shake his finger at me as I headed over to my Nana's cupboard for the cookie tin. "You're gonna get fat!" My Meme, who would always remind me that, "Amber's going to be thin like your father, and you're going to be fat like your mother and me." The female members of my family, who were constantly worrying about their weight, watching their figures and what they were eating.

These voices, combined with my desire to meet the "ideal" version of what I was being told women should look like, compelled me to eat less, exercise more, and spend much of my waking day thinking about food and how I could use it to manipulate my body to match the expectations that were put on it.

My whole eating disorder started on one long walk to the library, and my love of fitness activities grew from there.

But what was once a passion became an obsession.

My schedule became full of group fitness classes – any and all that I could take outside of school hours. I would wake up early in the morning to hit the gym before school, only to find myself back on the elliptical in the afternoons. If I had to work – a physical job that had me on my feet and occasionally moving heavy objects, I made sure that I walked over to the gym in time for evening exercise classes, usually Body Pump and Zumba.

These classes were my time to unwind, or so I thought. But during class, my thoughts mainly focused on judging myself and the other people in class. Those thoughts kept pushing me to try harder, move faster, lift heavier weights. No matter what I did, it was never enough. There would never be enough exercise classes to satisfy my compulsion to work out. I would never burn enough calories to feel good about myself. No matter how hard I tried, how hard I pushed myself, it was never enough.

My relationship with exercise, like my relationship with food, became extreme.

Early one evening, as the sun was setting, I took off from my mom's house to take a class at the gym. It was winter, and the roads were coated with a slippery ice. As my '94 Mercury Sable, Frankie (named for its hideous green color) wound along the back roads, my thoughts drifted away. Until, out of nowhere, a car backed out of a driveway, nearly slamming into me.

My instincts told me to step on the brakes to avoid getting hit. The snow tires on my car were not enough to keep Frankie from careening off the road and into a snow bank with a solid THUD. Safe but shaken, I slumped in the seat, grateful that I had not hit anything. As I put Frankie in reverse and started to pull out of the snowbank, I found that my car wasn't going anywhere. I was stuck. Shit. My first thought was, "My parents are going to kill me. I can't call them." Followed by, "How am I going to get to class?" and the brief consideration of walking the rest of the way in sneakers and shorts while the frigid wind chilled my bones.

From around the corner, a truck came and pulled over. A friendly and earnest man came out to ask me if I was alright, then took a look at the car.

"Need some help, miss?" he asked. I nodded feebly, unable to form words out of sheer embarrassment and shame. "Looks like you got caught on a rock under this snowbank. Lucky for you, I can get you out of here in no time." I thanked the man, relieved, while he got to work pulling my car out of the snowbank.

As soon as he had finished and driven away, after profuse thanks, I hopped back in the Sable and kept on driving to the gym, anxious to get my body moving and the fat burning. I remember walking in the door of the gym, dropping off my bags and changing out of my boots, and feeling like I was walking through a dream. Surely I hadn't just crashed my car? Surely I could just brush off my accident and get back to class. But something kept irking me throughout the whole class, distracting me from the movements, pushing me back from the front row to the third, where I shook and shimmied amidst a mind full of anxious thoughts

Those trips to the gym called to me like a beacon to a ship lost at sea. The gym was my refuge when the rest of my world was crazy. Here, I could just put on my headphones or pull out a book to drown out my thoughts. I could focus, and all that was there was the next movement, the next rep, the next mile.

Each Saturday, without fail, I would wake up early in the morning, put on my shoes and walk the mile and a half to the gym on an empty stomach, packing only a light snack for after my workout and water. (If it was raining, I'd drive).

Once I arrived, I'd settle into a 30-minute spin class – my least favorite by far, but the challenge assured me I was on the right track. Then we'd get into a Body Pump class, lifting weights to the sound of Chris Brown and company. After that was a kickboxing class and a cardio dance class, both high energy, getting the blood pumping before everyone went off to enjoy the rest of their weekends, weekends that I would spend exercising and starving.

I took each of these classes, back to back, with no break. Only when I was done with all 4 would I pull out my apple and start to eat. Even when my stomach cried for nourishment, even when my head throbbed and a cloud of blackness stung behind my eyes, I wouldn't reach for food. I could only eat, I only deserved to eat, once I'd worn my body out through exercise.

By the time I started school again in the fall, I looked like an entirely new person. My first day back, I received lots of compliments about my weight. "Shannon, did you lose weight? You look great!" "Wow, you look thinner! What have you been doing?" Just those meaningless, benign comments meant to make you feel good. Little did anyone know, little did *I* know, that they were feeding my growing eating disorder.

My school days that year started with Meteorology, a class in which I learned nothing. Perhaps that was the result of my preoccupation with my weight and counting calories, as all I can remember is our classroom breakfasts and how cold the room was, due to a window that never quite shut all the way, even in winter.

One of my classmates had brought in a toaster, and every morning, as class was in session, students would get up to toast Pop Tarts for breakfast. And while I wanted to be part of that group, part of the ongoing joke, my eating disorder would not let me eat anything other than an apple for breakfast. To that part of my brain, the part that revolved around numbers and ingredients, I couldn't justify the sugar and the calories, especially for something that had no nutritional value to it.

This was a huge part of my eating disorder - exclusion and watching other people eat. Because I was not eating, or at least not the kinds of food that everyone else partook in, parties and celebrations were more an agonizing opportunity to feel miserable, alone, and out of place than a chance to celebrate. As everyone else ate cookies or bagels or pizza, I would sit on the sidelines, watching with envy, wondering how they couldn't see that all of these foods were full of CALORIES. Weren't they afraid of getting fat? And any time someone asked me why I wasn't eating, I would justify my abstinence with my choice to be vegan, a choice that, in retrospect, was much more about restriction and eliminating more foods from my diet than about any kind of good it could do for my health, the planet, or the animals.

Lunchtime was a nightmare of a dance. There was not much in the lunch room that would constitute as healthy, and certainly nothing that fit the parameters I had set up for myself around food. In addition to the torture of watching everyone else eat and enjoy their food without the same neverending stream of commentary that accompanied every morsel I put in my mouth, going to lunch meant temptation.

Usually, I brought my own lunch: steamed veggies or salad without dressing or fruit. The only luxury I allowed myself, a meal that called to me like a siren on the shore as my stomach rumbled and growled with hunger, was a hummus and veggie wrap from the lunch line. When I realized how many calories were in the hummus, I asked the servers to put on half the amount. Then I asked them to just put veggies in my wrap - no hummus. The lunch ladies refused. By law, or whatever standards the school had set, they could not give me a lunch that didn't include some kind of protein. With some quick thinking, I eventually found a solution: they would put cheese on the side of my tray, which satisfied their requirements and which I would pass off to someone else upon sitting down at the table.

My days were structured around meals - or, more accurately, how to avoid them. I would spend hours preparing meals for my family, creating recipes from scratch or family favorites on request. And while I was preparing elaborate meals for them, I would steam myself some vegetables. If anyone asked, I had eaten while cooking, and this was just what I was eating so we could share a meal time together.

But they didn't buy it.

It was around October when my parents – my mom and stepdad, that is – started to ask me if I was anorexic. Of course, there was no way such a thing could happen to me. I was too good for that. I was only being healthy, trying to get in shape, I told them. There was nothing wrong with me. They were just jealous because, in a family of overweight people, I was the only one who looked good. I was the only one who was thin.

And it felt so good to be thin. I felt tall, lithe, and elegant despite my 5'2", stout stature. Much to my delight, I could fit into the clothes I saw on the models at the store. For once, my body was not bursting out of my clothes. For once, my ass fit in something that a normal person my age would wear. For once, I had everything I thought I wanted – those clothes hanging loosely off my body, the angles of my cheekbones. Finally, I was the beautiful girl I knew I could be but had never seen in the mirror.

But still, it was never enough. Weight would come off, and I'd wish to be thinner. When I looked in the mirror, all I could see was the stretch marks on my thighs, the ones that had developed at the young age of 12. I felt like a monster. Surely, there was something wrong with me to have stretch marks at such an early age. If only my stomach would be flatter, if only the space between my thighs was bigger, *then* I could be redeemed. Then other people would see me as beautiful. They wouldn't notice those stretch marks if I distracted them with angles and muscle tone.

As the months wore on and winter grew closer, I finally came to recognize that I had a problem, one that I wouldn't begin to fully understand for years.

I was on the bus to All State auditions (state-wide choral, orchestral, and band auditions) when it hit me that my parents were right: I had an eating disorder. As soon as the realization hit, I told my best friend, who was sitting on the bus seat next to me. Then I called my boyfriend, who lived a whopping 1,500 miles away in Florida. What difference it would make for him to know, I wasn't sure, but I trusted him with the updates of my life, and this seemed like a fairly significant update to relay.

The Sunday after auditions, I pulled aside my pastor, Lucy, to ask her if I could talk to her after the service was over. As the congregation poured out of the chapel and into the main hall for refreshments, I followed Lucy to her office. Once the door had clicked shut, I looked at Lucy and started crying.

Holding out a box of tissues, Lucy asked me what was going on. "Lucy," I choked out, "I think I have an eating disorder."

Now, the reason I had chosen to speak with Lucy in particular is because I knew that her daughter also struggled with anorexia. So not only was she someone I looked up to and admired in my community, but she was also the only person I knew who would understand what I was going through.

We spoke for an hour about my behaviors, about the eating disorder that was running my body, my mind, and my life, and we talked about a way to break the news to my parents. I was certain I couldn't do it. I couldn't let my parents down. I didn't want to feel I was even more of a burden to them than I already did.

I told my dad one evening when we were going out to my favorite Thai place in Derry, NH for dinner. I still remember sitting at that traffic light by the Wal*Mart, twirling my hair, working up the nerve to tell him. Then I just burst out with it, "Dad, I'm anorexic." In typical Dad fashion, he just stared out the window blankly, presumably compiling his thoughts. He eventually asked me what led me to that conclusion and what we should do about it. And when I try to recall the same situation with my mother, I honestly don't remember when or how I told her and what her response was like. That really says something, I think, about how attached I was to having my dad as a parental figure and how little significance I put on my relationship with my mother, which had vacillated back and forth my whole life.

By December, when I started treatment for my eating disorder, I had lost about a quarter of my body weight, leaving me at a bony 100 pounds. I was freezing all the time. The chill never escaped my bones. I would wear a spring jacket, a sweater, and a sub-zero winter jacket indoors, even to fall asleep at night, under a pile of every blanket we owned. I spent most of my time hunched in a ball to keep myself warm. My circulation disorder became more prominent, forcing me to wear gloves and a hat in the classrooms at school, a violation of school dress code, but an exception they were willing to make for a star pupil who was obviously struggling.

When I went to work, at a local florist, I spent hours in the cold, making kissing balls and wreaths for the holidays, fingers numb just minutes into the work. But I couldn't leave my job. I wouldn't. Despite everything that was going on in my life, despite the constant internal struggle and the pain I was in - both from hunger and from the numbness of my extremities - I could never admit weakness. I pushed through work the same way I pushed through my workouts - with grit and determination. I would not fail.

In January, I started therapy with a well-known eating disorder therapist, Monika, an author and recovered anorexic herself.

As a child of divorced parents, I'd spent most of my life in therapy, shooting the shit with counselors, never really diving into much of anything deep. My recollections of these counselors to date mostly revolved around building things - puzzles, models, Legos. Even then, I could not understand why my parents were driving so far to pay an old person to play with blocks with me.

There wasn't anything wrong with me, I told the counselors when they asked. At least that's how I felt. Life with divorced parents was normal, as far I was concerned.

With Monika, sessions were different. We talked about me. We talked about how I felt. We talked about my eating disorder. And it's with sadness that I tell you I cannot recount a single one of our conversations enough to relay any sense of detail, as my memories of this time were eaten away by my eating disorder, which did not allow me to focus on anything besides the hunger, a hunger that could never, not with any amount or any kind of food, be satisfied.

My eating disorder spoke in ways I could not. Despite being well-educated, the valedictorian of my class, my anorexia gave voice to a pain I couldn't bring myself to feel, let alone communicate.

Growing up in my family, the only emotion that was often expressed was anger. Anger at each other, at other people, at whatever was going on. Somebody, it always seemed, was angry about something. Abuse, as we would categorize it today, was commonplace in our household. It was not unusual to receive a spanking for not shutting up when we were told. It was not out of the ordinary to get yelled at for no good reason at all. And I cannot count the number of times I was chased around the yard with a wooden spoon.

So when I was experiencing this grief, the loss of my father that was not death but still the physical absence of his presence, I felt I had nowhere to turn. My mother would not understand. Surely my life was better without my father. What good was he anyway, keeping me from participating in the musicals I so desperately wanted to be a part of but couldn't because of his rules? Living so far away that I had but one friend near his home?

And my sister, my twin, was not in the least disturbed by his absence. The distance from my stepmother was exactly what she wanted: not to be pushed or asked to challenge herself, content to live in the status quo, getting by and doing things the "right" way, the way everyone else did.

I was all alone in my misery, and no one would understand it. No one would get me. And, not for the first time in my life, I was left to take care of myself. Yet the only way I knew how to was to make myself better in some way, which ultimately led to my eating disorder – a combination of personal improvement and the ultimate way for me to avoid feeling.

As a society, we are not brought up to share or express our feelings. When we are young, we are told, "Don't you get angry with me, young lady" or "Don't cry. Everything will be alright. Just wait and see." Our emotions are stifled because those around us don't know what to do with them, often because they, too, have spent a lifetime tiptoeing around what's been stirring inside of them.

For generations, our self-expression has been suppressed by well-intended parents with little time, knowledge, or patience to deal with our childlike tears and temper tantrums. There was no manual given to parents at birth that said, "Hey, when your kid is upset, let them be upset. You may want to take away their pain, but what you're really doing is denying them the opportunity to heal themselves by feeling their pain." They were given no dictionary filled vocabulary with which to say, "What's REALLY going on, sweetheart? Why are you upset? Talk to me. I want to help you. I love you, and I'm here for you."

And none of us is at fault for that. Our parents were doing the best they could with what they knew at the time, something I wish I understood much earlier than I did, as it would've saved me years of seeking to understand why my parents shut me out and shut me down.

We are taught to hush children, to expect perfect behavior from little people who do not yet comprehend logic and reason, who lack the ability to speak in fluid sentences and express themselves adequately.

And so this is the paradigm in which I grew up. This is the paradigm which I believe feeds addiction, eating disorders, and avoidant behavior that encourages us to do just about anything but FEEL what we are feeling. And this is the paradigm that I pray to God this book brings out into the open so it can be healed and laid to rest.

Winter 2008 - Deeper Down the Rabbit Hole

In early February, I had the opportunity to perform at Jazz All State. As one of the top-scoring altos in the state (auditions had been in the fall), I was placed in the Jazz A choir - a very prestigious honor, as the number of singers in the jazz ensembles was even more limited than the classical choirs, which I participated in the final three years of high school.

Jazz All State was held at Pinkerton Academy that year. Pinkerton is a large, semi-private school just a town away from where my mom lived.

The campus is huge, similar to that of a university, but fortunately we would be spending the majority of our time in one building - the Performing Arts Center, preparing for our concerts.

For three days, we would go over our music as a complete choral ensemble, working with some of the most skilled directors and accompanists, to hone each piece to perfection.

We weren't long into the first day of rehearsals when the room temperature became an issue for me. Due to my circulation disorder, the freezing cold New England winter temperatures, and the anorexia that dominated both my body and mind, I spent each day of rehearsal in a winter jacket and scarf. When my fingers started to go numb to the point that I couldn't turn the pages of my sheet music anymore, I knew I had to say something, as much as I dreaded the interruption or asking for any special favors.

I pulled aside one of the coordinators for the weekend and explained to them about my condition, asking them to turn up the temperature in the room. Because it was a medical condition, they had no choice but to oblige my request.

Even once the heat kicked on, my body was still freezing. Instead of turning up the temperature more, the coordinator took off in search of a pair of gloves. He returned with a pair of white gloves left over from the marching band season.

I felt like a fool. While my peers were laughing, making jokes with one another, and enjoying the whole experience, I was bundled up in layers, wearing tacky white gloves, my mind unable to focus on anything other than how cold I was and how many calories I had consumed that day. I wasn't sure I'd ever fit in again, and the feeling of depression, of being completely alone and misunderstood, washed over me as I sat huddled for warmth in my chair.

When the time came to audition for the solos in some of our pieces, I sat still in my chair, my thoughts conflicted. On the one hand, I really did want one of those solos, and I knew I could get it. The other singers in my section were nudging me to try out. But I couldn't get past the part of me that wanted to hide, that was afraid of standing in front of the choir, messing up, and being judged. I didn't want to mess up my improv, be off-pitch in my scatting, or give the group a chance to really LOOK at me and what I was wearing. I felt badly enough as it was, knowing that I would never be like these kids, never lead a life as carefree as their own.

That was a lot of my eating disorder: sitting around, watching other people enjoy their lives, and wondering why I couldn't do the same. My mind was flooded with constant questions. *Why is nobody else afraid of getting fat? How can they just eat whatever they want? Why can't I do that? Why am I like this? Why am I so different?* I wondered about their grades and the careers they'd have. I wondered if they had jobs and responsibilities at home. I wondered about anything that would give me an answer about why ME and not THEM.

I had resigned my life to my eating disorder, convinced that I would never recover. This was the message that was told to me by the books and by the doctors: chances of recovery are slim. Very few people fully recover from an eating disorder. Even if you get your weight under control, you will likely still struggle with food and thoughts about food for the rest of your life. You may never be normal again.

It was really no wonder then, that I kept falling deeper into the rabbit hole that was my eating disorder until someone gave me an alternative. (But more on that later).

Later that month, during February vacation, my family went on a cruise. My mom had been planning it for a while. She was excited to be taking us, as we had never been on a cruise before (my mother often rejoiced at opportunities to take us to do things my dad had not yet had the chance to).

The cruise was set to leave out of Port Canaveral in Florida, a 5-day excursion off the coast of Florida, down to Costa Maya and Cozumel, then back.

On board the ship, we settled in to our quarters. My sister and I were to share a room. We all split off to explore the ship, agreeing to meet outside our room before dinner so we could all head down to the main dining area together.

The food on board the ship was exquisite, to my delight and to my dismay. At the time, I had a very particular diet, refusing to eat certain foods and eating a purely vegan diet. The chef and wait staff were happy to accommodate these restrictions, crafting a truly beautiful and delicious dish at each meal. The part of me that loved good food could not resist such temptation, but the part of me that battled the eating disorder had me making up for it later.

Much of the time the boat was cruising, I spent in the gym. I would turn on my iPod, pounding the treadmill to the fast-paced and angsty sound of Paramore, my favorite running tracks, while watching the numbers on the treadmill: .3 miles. 22.8 calories burned. .4 miles. 30.4 calories burned. *God. Will it ever go faster?* I thought. *I need to burn those calories NOW!* My next meal was in just a few hours, after all...

If I wasn't in the gym, I was on the track that encircled the entire top deck. Again, I would turn on my iPod and lose myself in the music, oblivious to the curious stares of other cruise goers who, if we were in a cartoon, probably would have had those little question marks surrounding their heads. I mean, we were on a cruise ship, and while everyone else was in the pool smiling and having fun, here was this tiny, bony little girl, walking and walking and walking with deathly seriousness.

Of course, in addition to all that walking and running, the gym also had classes that were open to the general public, which I, of course, jumped on every opportunity to attend (because even on board that ship, I had an agenda for my day, which basically revolved around making sure that, no matter what happened, I wouldn't leave that cruise having gained weight).

If you've ever been on a cruise before, you know that it's not about being aboard a floating puke machine (I mean, really, who DOESN'T get nauseous when they climb on deck?); it's about the excursions.

So when we were in Costa Maya/Belize, we went on a bike tour and clear-bottom kayak excursion. As a group, we rode on the sidewalks through the streets of this small town, taking in the beautiful colors of the run-down and dilapidated homes. How could these people be so festive and colorful when their homes were just four walls and a simple ceramic roof? That was a question I didn't have the capacity to ponder, as my thoughts were preoccupied with calculating our mileage and approximately how many calories I was burning on this trip.

In Cozumel, I had what will probably go down as the worst vacation experience in life, EVER.

We were scheduled to go on a snorkeling adventure in the crystal clear waters off the coast of Cozumel. Now, this is typically not my idea of fun in the first place. If I am around water, I want to be splashing, swimming, and playing, not slowly meandering around, blowing through a tube and looking at fish who don't look that much different in real life than they do in photos from National Geographic. Suffice it to say I was not super excited about this excursion.

But, because this was a family affair, I went anyway. We got all suited up and ready to snorkel (or at least we pretended to be) and waited patiently for the guide to finish giving instructions so we could get in the water.

I jumped off the boat into the gorgeous ocean that looked oh-so-inviting, what with the rays of sun glinting off of its cerulean surface, and immediately regretted it. That water was COLD! (And I'm from New England!) We were in the goddamn Caribbean, and there I was, freezing my ass off. Not a happy camper.

I thought the initial shock would wear off and I could just swim around for a little bit, try to enjoy the underwater world and all. But less than 10 minutes after diving in, my teeth-chattering and blueish-purple skin being a dead giveaway of how cold I was, I was being pulled back onto the boat.

My parents sat me in a chair and covered me in towels. I put on every sweater we had on hand. What a sight that must have been for the other passengers: a girl layered up in sweaters and swathed in a mountain of towels in the warm tropical sun while everyone else was walking around in bikinis and boardshorts.

But this was what life was like for me with an eating disorder. I couldn't do what most people could. When I was volunteering, I would border on passing out, always having to ask myself if I would even be able to stand up for a few hours. When others were having fun and going off on adventures, I was left on the sidelines, alone and cold, with frantic thoughts about food. It is very hard to enjoy yourself when the only thing you can think about is how fat you are, how fat you'll be if you eat this or that, or how much weight you'll gain if you sit still for even a minute. You have to be up on your feet, moving around, moving your body. Otherwise, the fat will come back. Like kudzu in the south, it will creep up on you and take you over. Or at least that's what the voice in my head, the eating disorder, was saying.

Spring 2009 - The Downward Spiral

It had been a year and a half since I'd seen my stepmother. I only knew she still thought about me because of the cards she would send: from France, for birthdays, on special occasions. But still, in 18 months I had not seen the woman, and she hadn't extended an invitation for tea and biscuits either.

That's why it was a surprise when I suddenly caught the notion to come for a surprise visit.

At this point, my dad and I had standing date nights. We would go out for dinner somewhere, then go rollerskating together. We'd start out racing each other around the rink, each cheering the other on during fun rink games (but remembering that we were still in competition), and skate and chat together during couples skate, when only pairs of people could be out on the floor.

But this particular Friday, my dad was sick, which meant he canceled our plans. I was devastated. I had so been looking forward to seeing him again, to spending time together, catching up and telling him what was going on at school and at home. So when he texted me to let me know he was ill, I figured I'd bring our daddy-daughter date to him.

I got in the car and, without thinking, headed toward Newburyport. It was only once I'd gotten on the highway that I realized that I didn't know how to get to my father's house. In all the years we'd spent driving to and from school as kids, I'd never actually been paying attention. Amber and I usually sat in the back of the van, reading or singing along with whatever CD was playing. This realization prompted the first round of tears. I was so far removed from my father and his fiancée that I didn't even know how to get to where they lived.

Once I had their address (which I DID have memorized) in my GPS, navigating the roads was much easier, and as I got off the highway, the streets became familiar, memories flooding my consciousness.

As I drove down Water St., which, interestingly enough, turns into Water Rd. on the city line, I finally knew where I was headed: Mr. India, our family's favorite restaurant.

When Amber and I were younger, we would all go to Mr. India, each ordering our favorite dish. Aloo Gobi (cauliflower and potatoes in a red curry) for me and Steppy, Chicken Masala for Amber, and Chicken Korma for Dad. We'd sit together, huddled in a booth, Middle Eastern music playing in the background, while we sipped ice cold water and mixed our curries with steaming white rice.

As I stepped into the restaurant, those moments came rushing back, and I found myself nervous, unsure of what to do, ordering takeout alone from a place that once was the setting for many a family dining experience.

Figuring my father probably wouldn't be in the mood for solid food, I ordered some soup, and sat down to wait. Once the soup came out and I got back to the car, I called my dad. The phone rang. BRRRING BRRRING! My stomach did back flips. He picked up.

The words rushed out of my mouth, no longer hesitant, but anxious and hopeful. "Dad? I know you're sick and everything, but I really want to see you. I just picked up some soup and stuff from Mr. India. Do you think it would be OK if I stopped by the house for a bit?"

Silence.

"Let me check with Steppy. I'll call you back."

And so I waited in the parking lot for my answer.

"Yes."

The 7-minute drive from downtown Newburyport to Plum Island had never seemed so long. The marshes seemed to never end, their familiar and odorous smell wafting through my nostrils as I drove down the turnpike and onto the island. I crossed over the bridge, my heart climbing to my throat. The familiar beach town, where nothing had changed over the years, spanned the view in front of me.

When I parked in the driveway, I had the feeling I was a guest, not an inhabitant, of this residence, like I was meeting someone else's parents instead of my own.

The sign on the front porch said, "Enter in back." This was typical, something we did each winter to keep people from trekking snow through the living room. Instead, we would send people to the hallway in the rear of the house, where one could scrape their shoes on the mat and take them off before entering.

I walked around to the back door, taking in the change in the landscape. They had pulled out all the seagrass in the backyard. The walkway was no longer brick, but stone, wedged in the sand. Somehow, this felt significant. The simple, aesthetical changes to the home were representative of the changes in the nature of my relationship with my body and with my parents. The empty backyard, now devoid of a trampoline, reminiscent of a home without children. The crooked stones marking a path to the door struck me as being a bit like our topsy-turvy family dynamic, in which you can never be sure if you'll catch your footing when you make the next step forward.

I opened the door and walked in, pausing to stomp my boots on the mat, then pulled them off and put them in the lineup of shoes in the walkway. When I turned to open the door to the kitchen, I saw that my stepmom had already beaten me to it, throwing open the door and crushing me in a giant bear hug, the likes of which we'd never before experienced together. This commenced round 2 of tears, although this time, mine were shared by my stepmother, a woman whom I had rarely seen cry in our previous 10+ years of knowing one another.

She ushered me into the kitchen, where my dad was sitting at the table. I put down my bags and pulled out the soup, offering it first to my dad. On the stove were pots and pans all full of steamed vegetables, which Steppy had prepared to augment our meal. The subject of conversation, the words shared over that meal, are lost to me now, but that feeling of fullness, not from the food, but from the company of both of my parents, is something I'll never forget.

We talked for hours, late into the night. I was reminded of just how much I am like these two people, in terms of perspective and ethic. We all valued simplicity, choosing empty space and utility over knick knacks and tchotchkes. We all chose mainly plant-based diets, made sacrifices to be more environmentally friendly, composted, and recycled. We were all forward, radical thinkers, dreaming and scheming big about entrepreneurship, financial literacy, and personal responsibility. *These,* I thought, *are my real parents. The ones who raised me.*

And, in retrospect, I realize that the reason I felt that way is because much of what I've learned in my life I attribute to my stepmom, the woman who took it upon herself to teach my sister and me what schools, and my biological parents, would not, could not, or did not teach us. About how to manage your money, how to work hard to get what you want, how to be in integrity with your word. And so much of what she taught me shaped me, shaped me into someone who did not align with or resonate with what my mother and stepfather were preaching and teaching in their home.

Later that evening, I called my mother, who was not happy with me for staying out late and because of where I'd been. Against her wishes, I stayed the night. As we were setting up the pullout couch, I had the notion to stay with my dad and Steppy on a more permanent basis. I told them about this idea, and they asked me, as they were prone to

do, to make a list of reasons why this was a good decision, to weigh the pros and cons of living in each household.
So I did.

I made a list of all the reasons why I was like Daddy and Steppy and not like Mum and Dave. I made a list of all the reasons I didn't want to stay in New Hampshire, which included feeling like my eating disorder was exacerbated by my mom's presence, her constant questioning, and the judgment and criticism I received from her side of the family.

With that, my dad was sold. The only step left to take was to tell my mom. Which I kind of didn't do. And by that, I mean that I packed up my car and moved out of my mom's one day, letting her know only hours in advance, convinced she'd unpack my car or would use some other means to try to stop me. She was upset, of course, and issued an ultimatum, "Live here part time or don't come see me at all."

It seemed like I would constantly be in a battle of which parent I liked more, always exposed to their obvious distrust and dislike for one another. But in the battle for my life, I had to make the decision that was best for me. So I chose the parent with whom I shared more in common, who was less of a trigger to my eating disordered thoughts than the other, and that was my father.

Moving in with my dad, I'm convinced, was critical to my recovery. Sure, there were plenty of reasons why it could have thrown me off track (no friends in the area, farther away from school, stricter rules), but the consistency of having my parents show up and hold me accountable played a crucial role in learning to trust and take care of myself.

My dad was the one who watched me struggle to eat. He was there sitting with me in the dining area of Whole Foods while I anxiously spent an hour and a half eating a blueberry muffin, picking it apart, eating it crumb by crumb, crying because I thought I would get "fat". He and Steppy kept the fridge stocked with my favorite foods: fat-free vegan triple berry muffins, veggie sushi, and Hunan dumplings from Macro Vegetarian. They made me stir fry and sat down to eat it with me at dinner. At my mother's I was prone to cook my own food, along with a non-vegetarian option for everyone else.

This isn't to say, though, that living there was all family fun and games. Living with my dad and Steppy brought with it new challenges, like facing the void of emotional availability when trying to connect regularly with my dad. It was like he was OK talking about surface stuff, hearing about what was going on at school or whatever, but as soon as I started to share my feelings, really get into processing what was going on for me, he would shut down. It was as if a part of him fell through a trapdoor and got locked in there any time something emotional came up.

And Steppy was another story. For all of her love and support, she was also prone to criticism and control. She had a very particular way of thinking things should be done, and she wouldn't have it any other way. So if I was told not to over-exercise and she heard me lacing up my shoes for an early morning walk to the lighthouse at the asscrack of dawn or lightly bouncing on the floor to a muted workout video from Denise Austin circa '86 before school started, she'd be up the stairs in a heartbeat, turning off the VCR or shutting the door in my face before I could leave. This, for her, was a way of showing love and caring, not with words, but with actions.

That spring, Steppy invited me to travel to France with her, a follow up to our visit as a family in the summer of 2007. I was ecstatic. Steppy and I would fly over there, stay with a host family, and spend half our days studying à l'école (at school), half exploring Paris, eating croissants and crêpes. My dad would pay for my food. Steppy would pay for school and lodging, and my only responsibility was to pay for round-trip airfare from Boston to Charles de Gaulle. Thank god I'd been saving up for all those years.

The only caveat was this: "You have to be in a good place with food. We can't be worrying about you or having you wind up in the hospital overseas."

Done, I thought. I can do this. God, did I need motivation, because nothing so far was working. I so desperately wanted those voices out of my head, but I just couldn't figure out how to get them to stop. Maybe this was my chance. Maybe this trip would inspire me, hold me accountable. Maybe my desire to study abroad would be stronger than my impulse to starve, binge, and purge.

It wasn't long after the invitation was issued that it was withdrawn. Despite constant negotiating with my mother, she refused to give her permission to allow me to travel abroad. Not because of an issue with my passport, not because she didn't believe I'd be in a good spot in my recovery, but because my only traveling companion would be my stepmother. You'd think she was a villain, or at the very least, my mother's arch nemesis. My stepmom feared that as soon as I lifted off US soil and touched down on European ground, my mom would call the cops and report it as a kidnapping (because, at this time, Steppy was not legally married to my father. Just, you know, *engaged* for 7 years). This is literally the crap I had to think about. And they wondered why I was crazy.

I begged. I pleaded. I talked about how good it would look on college applications, on job applications, to show that I was well-rounded, well-traveled, and well-versed in not just one but two languages. I talked about how the French culture was around food. Maybe it would help me. My mom never acquiesced.

Dashed were my dreams of returning to France, and gone was the opportunity of a lifetime.
I really resented my mom in times like this, as it felt like she was always waiting to squash my hope of ever living a better life.

Not too long after, I was attending a vegan Meetup with Daddy and Steppy, as I had very few friends at the time, and absolutely none in Newburyport or Plum Island. Besides that, I often preferred the company of adults – less gossip and comparisons and more maturity than a bunch of teenagers.

We went to the Purple Onion, a small restaurant in downtown Newburyport. The food was atrocious. And besides that, despite knowing in advance that our group was vegan and explaining to them what exactly we could and couldn't eat, they still served us guacamole with sour cream in it. Of course, it looked off to me, so I asked about it. Why in the hell anyone would put sour cream in their guac is beyond me, but it made for a lot of pissed off vegans.

After our less-than-spectacular lunch, we made our way to the small theater on State Street that often showed those movies that you never see in large commercial theaters because no one really cares about them, save for the elderly population, who could frequently be seen walking in to catch an afternoon matinee.

But today they were showing Slumdog Millionaire, a film that had only recently come out, to rave reviews. And man, that movie lived up to its expectations. As the credits rolled and we filed out of the theater, I found myself dancing exuberantly to the bhangra music as I walked out of the auditorium.

That high was incredibly short-lived. Upon exiting the theater, I turned my phone back on, noticing that there were a couple voicemails and a text message from my mom, "Call me. It's about Lucy."

I've never really been one to take orders, but when you throw my pastor Lucy, who was struggling with cancer, into the mix, I couldn't dial my mom's number fast enough.

I pulled away from the group as my mom picked up the phone. "I'm sorry, Shannon. Lucy died this morning in the hospital from cancer."

My knees buckled underneath me, and my parents rushed over to see what had prompted the sudden outburst of tears. "She died," I told them. "Lucy died, and I never went to see her in the hospital. I never even sent her a *card*."

The group swarmed over, offering their condolences and uttering soothing remarks about how Lucy was "in a better place".

I didn't care if she was in a better place. She wasn't HERE. She wasn't among the LIVING. The woman I trusted perhaps more than any other, who held my secret in confidence until I was ready to tell my parents, had passed from this life and on to the next, and I hadn't done a damn thing to let her know how I much I loved and appreciated her for all she had done for me, all she had been for me.

I grieved for days. Grieve to this day, still. And the downward spiral continued. Disappointment piled on top of disappointment, and I drowned my sorrows with days of starvation, the pains of hunger a welcome relief from the pain of feeling.

That spring, I had the first of many epiphanies related to my recovery.

It was after an appointment with my nutritionist, Rhys. I was walking back to my car after another session that can only be described as a futile attempt to get me to eat more.

Our sessions usually looked something like this: Chitter chatter between me and Rhys, catching up on the goings on of the past week or two since we'd had an appointment. I would tell him, usually lie to him, about how my food intake was going. We'd draft up a meal plan to get me eating 2,600 calories a day, which was the number that had been decided on to help me gain back the weight I had lost (not that I was part of that decision-making process at all). I couldn't do it. I wouldn't do it. 2,600 calories was at least 2,000 more than I was eating on a daily basis, and there was no way in hell they could expect me to make that leap just like that.

So while we were creating this meal plan, I'd lie about the numbers. I'd tell him that my homemade Larabars were 300 calories when, in reality, they were only two. I told him I'd get popcorn, neglecting to mention that I'd pop my own at home to minimize the caloric impact of the oil popcorn is typically cooked in.

And while he was adding hummus to my veggie wraps and dressings to my salads, I'd be plotting ways to slash the calories, eat less, make substitutions, and subtract certain ingredients so I wouldn't be eating so much, too much being anything that made me feel full or was more than just the bare bones of what I could be eating. Eating too much meant I was losing control, losing my focus. If I kept it up, I'd be fat, and then no one would like me. All my hard work would've gone to waste, and then where would I be?

So on this fateful day, we had the routine visit, the same old conversation, yet this time, when I walked out of the office, a thought popped into my head: "The only person I'm hurting by not following my meal plan is me."

Rhys wasn't dying because I was cutting corners. My parents weren't losing hair over lack of nutrients (at least not literally, although they probably were metaphorically).

So while there was a part of my brain saying, "Hahaha, you silly fuckers, I'm not going to eat this at all! SCREW YOU! You can't make me do anything, I'm not really going to eat all of this," there was another part saying, "FUCK. I'm killing myself. And this isn't screwing anyone over except me."

That one epiphany didn't turn my life around. I still had a long way to go out of recovery, but it did get the wheels in motion in my mind. It was on another trip home from Rhys' office that I had quite a different experience, one that would shape me for years to come.

I was in the car with my mom, driving back to her house after a trip to see Rhys, when she started talking to me about my recovery. She told me that Dave was getting frustrated with how long the process was taking and about how much time it was taking to get me from appointment to appointment, as my treatment team was scattered across New Hampshire and Massachusetts, so each appointment took about an hour and a half of driving time in addition to however long the appointment was.

Now, honestly, when I think back on it now, I'm not entirely sure Dave was even the one with those concerns, as my mom had a penchant for using others as a scapegoat when she didn't feel comfortable shouldering the blame for her choices. But as a 16-year-old girl, I wasn't ready to face the fact that my mom found my recovery tiring and trying, so blaming Dave it was.

I have no recollection of how the conversation escalated. I can only presume that I was defending myself, saying I was doing the best I could, that they didn't know what it was like. But at some point in the conversation, my mom looked at me and called me a selfish bitch.

The world stopped. I was furious. My face burned with shame. And a part of me wondered if she was right, if I really *was* being selfish. Another part of me was indignant, knowing that I was not a selfish person in the least, thank you very much. If I was, I certainly wouldn't have spent so much time volunteering and taking care of others. Yet another part of me was hurt, wounded, and victimized, thinking, "What the hell? You're my MOM. I am trying to save my LIFE here, and you're worried about how much TIME it's taking? You sure didn't have a problem taking Amber to all those doctor's appointments years ago."

But then I guess it must've been easier back then, before my mom realized that she had two damaged children, before she'd spent hundreds of thousands of dollars on treatment and sleepless nights wondering if her daughter would die in her sleep or end her own life. It must've been easier to deal with a condition that was more understood, less volatile, and could be treated with medication, rather than my out-of-control eating disorder which only seemed to lead me deeper and deeper into a pit of despair. My hope for recovery was bleak, not just for me, but for those around me who struggled with seeing someone they love throw her life away.

I carried that shame and that label "selfish bitch" with me for years until I was finally able to recognize that the person who was wounded in that moment was not me. I was not the victim in that car. My mother was. Because what kind of pain must my mom have been in? What kind of stress must she have been under, to call her daughter a selfish bitch for wanting recovery, for wanting to survive?

No, I wasn't the only one struggling at that time. While I was struggling for me life, my parents were struggling to save their daughter.

Summer 2009 - The Summer of Crazy

Just three weeks before school was out for the summer, I was kidnapped by my parents and forced into a mental hospital.

I had just arrived home from school and was settling into my moon chair (the same one I'm in right now writing) to do my homework when I heard a car pull into the driveway. *Odd,* I thought. *Daddy and Steppy are already home.*

When I looked out the window, I saw my mom's Camry and both her and Dave climbing out of it. They walked in the front door and asked my dad, who did not at all sound shocked by their sudden appearance, "Where is she?" then walked down the hallway from the living room to my bedroom.

When they appeared in my doorway, I was a bit confused. Why were they here? Was this an intervention or something?

"Pack your bags. You're going with us," they said. Now I really did not like where this was going. I mean, I had just moved to my dad's and wasn't thrilled in the least with the notion of spending time at my mom's.

So I packed an overnight bag, grabbed my laptop, and hugged my other parents goodbye, while Mom and Dave led me out of the house.

They didn't say anything on the 45-minute drive back to New Hampshire, which really irked me, as I was still wondering what was up.

When the car stopped, I realized we weren't at my mom's house at all. "Hampstead Hospital," the building said.

"You're here to meet with a psychiatrist," my parents told me.

Umm... ok, I thought. *Wouldn't it just have been easier to send me here after school instead of making me drive all the way to Plum Island and back?*

I walked into the therapist's office and sat down on the rather uncomfortable leather sofa to answer her questions.

"Shannon, do you know why you're here?"

"Yeah," I said. "Because I'm fucked up, have anorexia, and my parents want me to get better."

"Ok. Do you know where you are?"

"Not really. They just told me I'm here to talk to the psychiatrist so I can get help."

"Ok, honey. You're at Hampstead Hospital. This is an in-patient psychiatric facility. Your parents have registered you to join us for a few days in the Young Adults ward, where we can keep track of you and where you can get the help you need."

I could've died from embarrassment. I had an EATING DISORDER, not mental problems! I couldn't be here. This wasn't where I belonged. And I didn't have a few days to spare for shootin' the shit with some crazies. Just tomorrow I was due to be presenting a speech to the student body to become the student liaison to the school board! How was I supposed to do that from the hospital?

So I did what I did best: Run away.

I stood up and walked right out the front door, surprised that no one even tried to stop me.
I started walking down the road, not entirely sure of where I'd go, but knowing I couldn't stay THERE.

A car pulled up alongside me, on the other side of the road. Dave leaned his head out the window. "Shannon, get in the car."

"No."

"Shannon, this is going to be so much easier for everyone if you just get in the car."

"NO!" At which point I started running, cutting down a side road, looking to find a place, any place to hide. I felt like a fugitive on the run from the law. I was humiliated. Who knew who was out there watching me, watching us, while my parents chased me down so they could lock me up? I have nightmares about it to this day.

I ended up turning down a side street into a beautiful neighborhood filled with idyllic houses, homes that probably housed families much more sane and normal than mine. I heard a car behind me and jumped into the hedges, curling up into the fetal position.

And this is where Dave found me, picked me up, and forced me into the car, returning me to my new home at Hampstead Hospital. Dave dragged me into the building with me fighting every step of the way, holding onto the glass doors, kicking, screaming, throwing my arms around in the air, looking every part the crazy my parents and the administrative staff thought I was.

They checked me into the hospital, where a nurse escorted me to the young adult's wing. I ignored my parent's goodbyes, resenting them with every ounce of my being for doing this to me, for locking me up like some crazy person.

The attendant took me into a room and strip searched me, pulling the shoelaces out of my shoes, taking my earrings away from me, checking my tongue and belly button for piercings I could use to stab myself or someone else. They left my computer with my parents, as well as my spiral bound notebooks, lest I should remove the binding and use it choke myself, which, when it dawned upon me where I was and what was happening, seemed like a really appealing option.

That night, when I went to brush my teeth, I found that the bathrooms had no mirrors. When I asked the nurse why not, she said that they couldn't take any chances with materials that someone could use to hurt themselves or others. Apparently, a girl had once broken the mirror with her fist and used it to cut herself, at which point they removed all the mirrors from the bathrooms.

What kind of place had my parents committed me to? And who was I going to meet in the morning when the wing was awake?

The next morning when I came out into the common area by the bathrooms, I saw a bunch of young people. They looked pretty normal, except for this heavy girl with cuts all over her arms and face. Hesitantly, I sat down at one of the tables.

"What are you here for?" the girl next to me asked.

"Because my parents are jerks," I replied.

"But really," she pressed, "What did you do? Cut yourself? Take pills?"

"I'm just anorexic," I said.

The girl seemed disappointed.

The kids around the table started to introduce themselves, telling me their name, age, and what got them committed to Hampstead Hospital. There was a little girl, about 9 years old, who was there for depression. The girl next to me had tried to kill herself. The guy across the table was from a foster home and had anger management issues that got him kicked out and locked up. The big girl with the cuts was there for cutting and raging outbursts that I would later become all too familiar with.

I didn't belong there. All I had was an eating disorder. I wasn't crazy or anything. I wasn't hurting anyone.

And that's the thing about eating disorders: while they're categorized by mental illness, they're so difficult for most people to understand. Because while we've all been a bit depressed or anxious at times, it just seems incomprehensible that you'd want to deprive yourself of food all day.

When we look at the word "anorexia," it means "loss of appetite." But we don't specify the appetite. It's not that I didn't feel hungry during the day. It's not that I didn't want to eat or didn't salivate thinking of my favorite foods, but that I felt like I *couldn't* eat. Not eating was my way of being in control. It was my way of numbing the pain of trying to be perfect all the time –and despite what seemed like a lot of external success, I never felt good enough.

Anorexia was a way of slowly killing myself. It was a way to put me out of my misery and distract me from my pain. And that doesn't make sense to most people. Why would you hurt yourself more so you could hurt less? But in a twisted way, it made complete sense to me: I could feel the pain of hunger, or I could feel the pain of overwhelm, of fear, of anger, of hurt, of rejection, of abandonment, of so many things whose weight seemed to be bearing down on my body.

So it was symbolic that I was losing weight. If I could lose weight, if I could be lighter, maybe then I wouldn't feel so heavy. Maybe then I wouldn't feel so burdened and encumbered by life.

That's why I think it's not about trying to fully understand eating disorders, but rather draw parallels to other conditions and make analogies to more common life circumstances so we can at least begin to understand, and thus have some more compassion for, eating disorders. I don't expect anyone who hasn't struggled with ED to get what it's like to feel so bogged down by reality, but if I can give you a glimpse or an inkling of what it's like by relating it to your own life, I've done my job and maybe I'll finally be able to sleep at night.

After breakfast, we were released from the wing and walked a whopping 10 yards to the group therapy room, where we set our goals for the day and had a discussion on whatever topic the program coordinator had selected for that day. Per my usual MO in these kind of group situations, I ended up hijacking the conversation and teaching the class myself, asking my peers questions and lending an empathetic ear for the answers.

The recreation advisor who led the groups – and spent the most time with the residents – pulled me aside once group therapy was over.

"What are you doing here?" he asked.

"I have an eating disorder. There's something wrong with me, and my parents want to fix it."

He shook his head in disbelief. "You should be teaching here, not staying here. I don't know what got you into this place, but it won't be for long. You've got your head on straight. Whatever's going on, you'll pull through it. I know you will."

And he was right. Three days later, I was released from the hospital with well wishes and, for the first time since my diagnosis, hope for recovery.

The second time I ended up at Hampstead Hospital, I called the cops on myself.

I was at my dad's house one night and we were having an argument about god knows what – probably our millionth argument to date, usually stemming from my dad's inability to connect and relate with what was going on for me.

The result of our argument was my teetering on the edge of my safe zone, my mind drifting into two distinct possibilities for what I'd do next: take the car and drive away or take the car and run it off the road.

I knew in that moment that I couldn't be at home anymore, because, if I was, I'd do something stupid. I'd do something I'd regret – if I lived to regret it.

So I made a split decision and called 911.

The cops arrived with an ambulance. I greeted them at the back door. My parents ran upstairs after hearing the sirens in the yard, clueless as to what was going on.

They looked at me. "Shannon, why are the cops here?" I stared them down, "Because I don't feel safe, and they're going to take me away."

They started asking why I didn't tell them, why I would just call the cops instead of letting them know that I needed to get away, why I would waste the money on an ambulance when they could drive me to the hospital themselves.

Before I could answer, before I could convey to my parents just how scared I was of what they might say to me, the ways in which they would invalidate my feelings, brushing them off as just another silly thing my eating disorder concocted, the medics started asking questions, pulling me away from my parents, and strapping me onto a stretcher.

As they loaded me onto the ambulance, I felt relief start to settle in. I was on my way to safety. I was about to be reunited with the only people in the world who understood me, the other kids who knew what it was like to struggle, to want to hurt themselves, to feel unsafe around their families, the people who were supposed to love them, protect them, and care about them the most.

On the way to the ER, the EMTs questioned me. As was usual in this scenario, the very compassionate medics asked why a girl like me would want to end her life and throw it all away.

While it was very sweet of them to ask, it just deepened the feeling I had that no one would ever understand me outside of that mental hospital. How could these people not see I was dying on the inside already? What did it matter if I was killing myself on the outside? How could they not see the pain I suffered through day in and day out? They didn't know what it was like, hearing voices in your head telling you you're not good enough, forcing you to starve, to exercise, to do anything and everything you could to be better, in the hopes that someday you'd be good enough, even when you knew you wouldn't.

The ride to the emergency room was a short one. When I arrived at the hospital, my vitals were taken and I was given a room with a bed to lay down in. Doctors and nurses came in to ask me the same questions over and over. The lights were too bright to sleep. I wondered where my parents were, what they were doing, if they were talking to each other and wondering what in the hell they'd ever done to deserve a kid like this. If they were wondering how often this would happen. Or if they were maybe even wondering when I'd just go through with it and end the pain and suffering for us all.

Sometime early in the morning, after I'd been laying in the ER bed for hours, restless and unable to sleep, listening to the hustle and bustle outside my door, my dad came in, looking haggard, holding in his hand a coffee and a donut. I reminded him that donuts weren't vegan. He reminded me that it was 3 o'clock in the morning and Dunkin' Donuts was the only place where he could get coffee and something to eat.

We looked at each other after that, wondering without words what was going to happen next, when this was all going to stop.

Finally, the EMTs came in again to load me back onto the ambulance so we could make our way to Hampstead Hospital. I said goodbye to my dad, and he left for work, leaving me just as alone as I felt.

You know things are a little bit off in your life when you feel more at home in a psychiatric facility with girls who tear off their skin and break open windows with dresser drawers than while living with your family.

It was after my second stay in the young adult's quadrant when I decided I'd rather stay in there with all the other crazy people than go home to the people who constantly harped on me and badgered me with questions without ever stopping to actually listen for the answer. At least, in the hospital, there were people who understood me, who not only listened to me, but HEARD me.

Let me just get on my soapbox for a second here:

There's something to say for being in a place where everyone has no choice but to admit that they're at least a little fucked up. There's something liberating about baring all your flaws and insecurities to strangers who aren't afraid to share their own. Whether they had overdosed on pills, cut their wrists, or thrown Godzilla-like temper tantrums in their foster home, all of these kids had a story to tell, and they weren't ashamed to share it. After all, how often are we given the opportunity to open the doors and shine a light on all of our deepest, darkest secrets? In a world that shuns imperfection, living in a place full of it was a blessing of sorts.

So often, in the "outside world", we put a wall, a barrier, around our feelings and our experiences. We hide behind these walls and pretend that we are faultless, flawless beings, when, deep down, we feel hurt, broken, and empty. We feel pain we have no idea how to express, because, when everyone else is hiding behind their mask of perfection, we feel more than vulnerable even thinking about taking off our own.

off soapbox

That's why, when I found myself in the car heading home with my father just a few days after my arrival at the hospital, I felt like someone had taken away my rock, my security blanket, my real support team. As we sped down the highway back to the beach house and my dad asked me what it was going to take for me to get better, I was reminded of just how unsupported I felt in my real life, outside of the hospital. I tried to explain to my dad what I hope this book is explaining for you: how an eating disorder works, what my thoughts were like, how difficult it was just to make it through the day, constantly having to battle my own mind, which was torn between hurting me and wanting to recover.

Since I was in a moving car, hurtling down the interstate at 70 miles an hour, I had no way to escape. No way to avoid his questions, the sideways looks. And somewhere in that twisted and screwed up mind of mine, I got so overwhelmed that I could not think straight. I reverted to my primitive self, the part in me that is like the part in all of us that, when hurt, wants to strike back at what is hurting it, even if the pain is not physical. Which is how I ended up punching my dad square in the arm.

I just wanted him to stop. Stop talking. Stop asking questions. Stop not understanding. Stop thinking it was easy to just eat. Stop reminding me of just how much I was fucking up everyone else's life along with my own.

He was pissed. I unbuckled my seatbelt and cowered in the small space underneath the glove compartment and in front of my seat. He yelled at me to get my ass out of there and back onto the chair before he turned the car around and brought me back to the hospital. I dared him to.

This is a drama that, looking back, unfolded plenty of times between my father and me. Because he often did not understand, because he left the parenting to Steppy, left all communication to his children to my stepmother, I often provoked and antagonized my dad, just to get a response out of him. Because, as a child, dying for attention from her father, any response is better than no response at all.

Later that month I was on a bus to New York City with a dozen or so friends and chaperones from my youth group at church.

Why my parents let me leave the house to go to the city with people who knew very little about my eating disorder and how to handle it is beyond me.

Yet there I was, in New York, staying at a hostel with folks I've pretty much grown up with since I was 12 years old, and while our schedule was action-packed with fun, touristy activities, my focus was almost entirely on food, diverting only to pay mind to my constant fatigue, which wore me down as we walked all over the city.

In the mornings, our hostel provided a continental breakfast. Everyone was allowed one of everything: 1 juice, 1 milk, 1 cereal, 1 bagel, 1 muffin, 1 apple, 1 banana, 1 orange. As we walked through the breakfast line, we each loaded our trays up with one of each, figuring that if we didn't want it, someone else would. At the very least, it would make a good snack for later.

Because my options were limited as to what I would actually eat, I ended up munching on an apple and a starchy banana for breakfast, a couple more stashed in my bag for later in the day (which I actually ended up handing out to the homeless while we toured various parts of NYC).

The reason this story sticks out in my mind isn't because of what I ate, but because of how the whole trip felt. It was the first time I really went out with a group of people and felt like I didn't belong with them at all. These people were my family. We shared our lives together every Sunday and at sleepovers, outings, and on mission trips. And yet I felt like I was removed from the group, an outsider, a casual observer, watching everyone else enjoy themselves while I looked on, wondering what it would feel like to belong, to be carefree, to just enjoy myself without worrying about whether I would get fat or not, and what that would mean for me.

There's one picture of this trip that stands out for me, and it is of a tiny, little me, size 0 shorts hanging off her waist, looking in the window of a bakery at one of New York's famous cheesecakes, something you wouldn't have been able to get me to touch, let alone eat. And a pang of heartbreak echoes through me as I recall just how much I wanted to be able to enjoy that cheesecake. I wanted to eat pizza with my friends. I wanted to visit the M&M store and snag a handful to snack on on the subway. I wanted to go to the restaurant in Chinatown and order chicken fingers and white rice rather than plain, steamed vegetables.

So much of our culture, so much of our connection with others, revolves around food. And so when we remove that fundamental element, it's like being lost. You have no idea how to connect with other people. Parties, holidays, and gatherings become a war zone. Internally, you are battling the part of yourself that just wants to relax, enjoy, and connect vs. the part that believes it is bad, wrong, selfish to eat, the part that thinks that if you gain weight, something bad will happen.

And so surrounded by friends and family in the Big Apple, I felt incredibly alone, isolated, and depressed, a smile only curving up on my face in the rare moments when I was able to find relief from the voice that was constantly urging me to do more, move more, burn more calories, eat less food, lose more weight.

This feeling of being alone in a group plagued me for years as I struggled through social events where everyone but me, it seemed, was indulging in dessert, pizza, or some other food that was, to my eating disorder, untouchable.

Fall 2009 - Unexpected Consequences

Sometime in the late summer, I started experiencing extreme pain whenever I sat down and I started spotting blood in my underwear. I hadn't been menstruating since the fall, and my body was incapable of ovulating due to insufficient body fat. I knew there had to be something else going on. Every time I laid on my back to do crunches, I was fighting through the pain, which felt like my tailbone was ripping through my skin every time I raised my body up and then down. When I got on my bike to go into town, even the thick, padded cushion on my seat couldn't protect me from that jabbing sensation.

When I went to the doctor for my weekly check-in, I asked about it. Almost immediately she had an idea of what it was: a pilonidal cyst.

Of course, my mind hears "cyst," and I'm like, "Great. Cancer. Yet another illness that will make me die faster."

But this was a different kind of cyst, one that actually makes me, someone who secretly loves gross and grody stuff, cringe. No, this benign cyst was not a sign of cancer or any other medical problem. It was a harmless hairball that was growing inside my body. AWESOME.

The bleeding was because the cyst was close to the surface, otherwise it likely would have gone undetected.

When I asked about how to remove it, my doctor recommended a surgeon; A male surgeon, who would later be checking out my butt crack while I was doped up on anesthesia.

Due to my low weight and lack of body fat, the procedure had to be put off. So I was faced with yet another ultimatum to gain weight: get this thing removed, or stay at the same weight and live with the constant thought of a giant hairball in my ass. FUCK MY LIFE.

The part of me that just wanted to get better and not deal with this kind of shit got me to eat a little more, gaining enough weight to make the surgery possible late in the summer, just weeks before school started back up. In addition to the utter humiliation of explaining to people what my surgery was for (because, really, who can talk about a hairball in their ass crack with dignity), I was also subjected to sitting on a donut-shaped inflatable cushion wherever I went, which made questions about my condition completely unavoidable.

It was just after this surgery that I was enrolled in a group program for teens in Nashua, NH called Directions. I'm telling you, I have no idea how my parents found this place, but they couldn't have done that much research on it, or they would have thought twice about sending me in with a bunch of teenage delinquents.

The group was meant to keep me out of trouble in the afternoons after school was out. I was required to drive myself an hour from Plaistow to Nashua so I could participate in a 2.5-hour program, then drive an hour and a half home. Yeah, all that driving would keep me out of trouble, for sure.

The first day I was due in Nashua, my mom drove with me to sign me in, talk to the therapist there, and meet the program leaders. The place looked nice. There were a bunch of kids my age hanging out in the living room, the kitchen was well-stocked with Clif bars, which we were free to grab and snack on at any time, and there were two other rooms: one for group therapy and one for private sessions with the doc.

After my mom felt like she'd gotten a good feel for what the place was about, she left, leaving me alone with a hippie-looking Buddhist with a bald head and Tom's loafers, a seriously cute therapist, and a bunch of kids who must have been a least a little bit as fucked up as I was, in order to be sentenced to time in that afterschool prison.

I went into the living room and started looking around, trying to gauge who I'd be spending my after school hours with. This was when Joe – the hippie group facilitator – called us all into the group therapy room. We went around the circle, introducing ourselves and sharing with the group what had brought us to the program. As the other participants started sharing, I began to feel, once again, dreadfully out of place.

The thought "Who the hell recommended this place?" crossed my mind at least once.

The group was mainly comprised of a bunch of teen males who struggled with either anger management issues or drug and alcohol abuse. There was one other girl my age in the group, a self-proclaimed sex addict. *Looks like I'll fit right in.*

The circle came around to me, and I shared with the others that I had an eating disorder. The group stared at me like I had three heads. Apparently it is much more relatable to be an addict than to be anorexic.

As the week wore on, the group forgot that I was a social pariah and started to accept me as one of their own. We all laughed together one session when Joe called on one of the guys to give his insights on some lesson we were discussing, and the guy gave a real roundabout, bullshit answer because he was stoned out of his mind. Joe asked if he was under the influence. The kid's head rolled about as he vehemently denied such a claim. We laughed harder.

Apparently there is solidarity in being part of a group of misfits and outcasts.

One afternoon we were going for a walk through the park that was just across the way from the facility. As we were walking, we formed clusters, and in those clusters, we started sharing the juicy details of our life stories, the drama that brought us to Directions. As it would turn out, many of my "friends" were either gang members or direct descendants of gang leaders. This, I was sure, would improve my street cred in the future, to have acquaintances who are closely connected to the Bloods and the Crips.

At the end of the week, I was hanging out with my mom, who asked me how the program went. I regaled her with stories of the previous week and shared my excitement for returning the next. She dis-enrolled me from the program, making a mental note to let my psychiatrist know what kind of tomfoolery is happening, so he can be sure not to recommend Directions to any of his other patients.

There are so stories, so many memories that center around my addiction to fitness, my drive to lose weight and burn calories through more exercise than could ever be considered healthy.

I have pushed myself so hard in bootcamp classes that I puked, cycled until I saw spots in my eyes, and walked until I couldn't feel my legs anymore. And as I write this, I grieve the moments I lost due to my obsession with food, weight, and exercise, because this eating disorder robbed me of what was left of my childhood, leaving me to face a lifetime as an adult without ever having had the chance to be a child.

I'm not sure how long the cycle of exercise bulimia would've lasted had I not been forced to stop it.

As part of my recovery, I was forced to show up for weekly check ins with my doctor. These appointments were where I experienced probably the most fear around my eating disorder.

The visits would start with a weigh in and checking of the vitals. The nurses had me step on the scale backwards in my dressing gown so that I could not see the weight, although that didn't keep me from hearing the click as the weights on the scale fell into place.

My weight was never revealed to me, but I could tell whether I had gained weight or lost weight from the way my doctor, Dr. Sheehan, spoke to me. If she seemed concerned, I was losing weight, and I knew I was on "the right track" - or so my eating disorder said. If she congratulated me on my progress and started a conversation about how I was feeling, I knew I was in dangerous territory, having gained weight. These visits to the doctor's office often stirred up thoughts of restriction, as I couldn't bear the thought of gaining weight.

Even now, I can't tell you what was so bad about gaining weight. I knew I had to. I knew my life depended on it, but somehow it also seemed to me that if I gained weight I would die. It was an irrational fear, which is why I believe that eating disorders aren't about the weight so much as what they're protecting us from. If my eating disorder was speaking for me, then gaining weight meant I'd lost that avenue for expressing myself, and that I'd be right back where I'd started, not getting whatever it was that I so desperately needed.

Dr. Sheehan also used these visits to warn me of the dangers of an eating disorder. She told me stories of patients whose esophaguses were burned by bile, whose knuckles were permanently scarred from purging, whose teeth were rotting from the acid. I ignored her stories, as my bulimia of choice centered around exercise, diet pills, diuretics, and laxatives.

It wasn't until late summer, when Dr. Sheehan ordered me to stop going to the gym, that I finally started listening. My heart, once healthy and vital, was slowing down to an unhealthy, uneven rhythm. My heartbeat was so weak, so quiet, that it took several nurses, my mom the EMT, and the doctor to measure my heart rate. With my heart in this condition, exercising with the intensity I was used to would put me at risk for a heart attack. And although I was slowly wasting my life away through starvation and purging, I knew I didn't want to die.

You might think that those who have eating disorders have a death wish, as they have the highest mortality rate of any mental illness: about 20% of anorexics die from eating disorder-related causes or suicide. But the truth is: I didn't want to die. And I don't think most anorexics do. Death just seems like a preferable option to feeling the pain inside.

When I got that call from my doctor, when I was on that table as they monitored my heart rate with an EKG, I felt so scared. All I wanted was to be thin, or at least that's what my mind told me. What I really wanted was to feel safe, loved, and secure. I wanted somebody to finally appreciate me for who I was instead of what I could do for them. I'd spent years trying to live up to other people's standards and gain their approval, but none of it was ever enough. I was never enough.

And now I was dying because of it. I was literally dying for acceptance.

Listening to my doctor's orders, and fearing for my life, I cut back on the exercising, choosing to walk (the only safe exercise I was allowed) instead.

Being unable to exercise really fucked with my eating disordered brain, which wanted me to be in continuous motion, moving quickly and efficiently so as to burn as many calories as possible. So when the no exercising mandate came into effect, throwing a monkey wrench in my eating disorder's plans, my compulsion took a new turn: binge eating. If I couldn't exercise while I starved myself, I wouldn't do it at all.

I started my senior year hauntingly thin with hardly a friend to call my own.

Over the previous year, I had pushed away anyone and everyone who tried to get close. I didn't want them to see my struggle, didn't want them to witness my weaknesses.

So I resumed my habit of spending my lunch periods in the teachers' lounge, opening up a can of Amy's chili or soup with a can opener I had brought myself, slowly spooning, chewing, and swallowing each bite as I finished English papers, math homework, or projects for one of my many extracurriculars.

I built a friendship with one of the teachers in there, a gentle giant of an English teacher, who seemed concerned about my eating habits, but never said much about them. He let me eat in there and do my work, keeping an eye on me in the meantime.

On the rare occasions when I did venture into the lunchroom, I found myself sitting with a group of classmates from French, kids who, in retrospect, I would consider to be really good friends, not that I knew it at the time or really accepted and appreciated their friendship.

In October of my senior year, one of these "friends" got in a wee bit of trouble for a book he wrote that was leaked for NaNoWriMo (National Novel Writing Month).

This guy wanted to participate in NaNoWriMo, but was struggling with an idea of what to write about that would make up 50,000 words. He eventually decided that if he wrote about the 350+ students in our senior class, he'd hit the mark.

What this young man ended up writing was a real world equivalent of Lindsay Lohan's "burn book" in the movie "Mean Girls".

I was out of school for a dentist's appointment the morning that the announcement was made to the entire senior class.

When I returned to school, my friends pulled me aside to let me know what was going on. They told me my friend was in trouble. I ducked outside to give him a call before heading to my next class.

"Are you alright?" I asked.

"I'm fine," he responded.

After school, I gave him another buzz on my way to my babysitting time, itching for details. He gave me none, only the desperate plea, "Don't read it, Shannon. I didn't mean it. If anyone sends it to you, just don't open it."

But curiosity has always been a driving factor in my life, so when a link to the PDF showed up in my Facebook inbox, I couldn't help but click the link.

Write there, smack in the middle of the alphabet, was my entry. An entire page, the longest entry in the book, outlining how I was only top of my class because I refused to take APs in subjects I didn't give a rat's ass about, how my eating disorder was a fraud to get attention and look good, and how I wasn't genuine in my interactions with other people. On top of that, I got the lowest "rating" in his entire novel: -infinity + 1. Meaning, in his mind, I was the worst person on the planet. Worse than the worst.

All of this, coming from a "friend".

At that point, I was really glad I didn't have a lot of close friends, because I didn't need even more people beating my self-esteem into the ground.

About a month after the burn book debacle, I met the man who would become my saving grace, Jason, a man whose praises I will never stop singing til they scatter my ashes off the southern coast of France years and years from now.

We met through the raw food community, and I was thrilled to be meeting someone who lived close by and was interested in the same branch of raw that I was (Doug Graham's 80/10/10 diet, a diet comprised mainly of raw fruit and leafy greens).

Over time, Jason became so much more than my raw food buddy. He became my mentor, my guide, and my life preserver.

J taught me the power of my thoughts and introduced me to the Law of Attraction, which is the idea that our thoughts create our lives. Whatever you focus on, wherever your thoughts go, consciously or unconsciously, that's what you make manifest in your life.

And considering that my thoughts were a bit deranged (or, perhaps, fairly normal in this day and age), I was manifesting some pretty awful shit.

The reel of thoughts in my mind sounded a little something like this: "I'm fat." "I'm stupid." "This will never work." "I'm going to die." "No one loves me." "No one understands me." "I hate my life." "I hate my body." So on and so forth.

As you can imagine, what I was bringing to life with my thoughts was a death sentence. I was creating and feeding my own eating disorder with these thoughts.

The first time I met Jason in person, we went running, rock jumping, and tree climbing at the Ipswich River Wildlife Sanctuary with his friend, Chris. Upon our return from our adventure, we settled into a low-fat raw vegan delicacy: a potently sweet and calorically dense combination of fresh, ripe permissions, Medjool dates, and bananas.

I indulged in more than I had planned on, my never-ending appetite a match for two, active, grown men. I felt terrible. The entire time we were supposed to be enjoying our meal, I was calculating in my head how many calories I was consuming, thinking about how I was over my limit for the day, and it was late enough in the evening that I wouldn't have time to make up for it.

I hated myself. Despised myself. Was disgusted with myself and my actions.

I had not only binged, I'd done it in front of people I admired and respected. New people whose friendship I hoped to garner over time. And now I'd ruined it by showing what I really was: a greedy, fat pig (or at least that's what my eating disorder told me).

Fortunately, neither Chris nor Jason saw me as the fat pig I deemed myself to be.

As I spent more time with Jason, I learned more and more what it felt like to be unconditionally loved and accepted by another human being, as Jason only saw the best in me and held the highest intentions for me. He quickly became my most trusted confidante, the person who could hold space for the myriad negative thoughts that consumed my mind without trying to get me to change them. The only thing Jason did was reflect back to me my beauty, my strength, and my power.

My friendship with Jason would become the pivotal point in my recovery.

Winter 2009 - Ending It

What do you do when you've got time to kill?

I arrived in Exeter early for my appointment, so I had some time to visit my favorite natural foods store, The Blue Moon. Upon walking in, I noticed that the café had a raw cheesecake on display. WIN. Excited to see such a delicacy for sale, I bought myself a slice and devoured the whole piece with vigor. Only after I had cleaned my plate and walked out of the store did it hit me that the raw cheesecake was full of calories, of fat grams upon fat grams, that I couldn't afford to spare.

I went to my car and grabbed my iPod, prepared to go for a nice, long walk around town to burn off what was about to become excess fat on my body. But, as I walked, my mind grew more paranoid. I felt nervous, like at any moment something bad would happen to me because I had eaten too much in one sitting, those calories burning a hole in my stomach. Before long, all I could think about was how disgusting I was, what a horrible person I was, how I had no self-control. My thoughts spiraled downward until I hated every ounce of my being, convinced I was no better than dirt, that I deserved to die.

I frantically texted my parents, telling them I didn't want to live anymore, that I was going to jump off the falls in downtown Exeter so they didn't have to deal with me anymore. I wouldn't be a burden on anyone. I wouldn't have to struggle with this eating disorder. I would finally be free. They would finally be free of me.

I walked and I walked as my mind raced. I wanted so badly to end it all, all the suffering that governed my days, the obsessive thoughts that overwhelmed my mind, and I was nervous as all get out about actually ending my own life. I didn't want to, but the compulsion was so strong. 'Do it,' my depression was telling me. 'Just end it all. No more worrying. No more bingeing. No more weight. You'll be free. You won't ever make a mistake again.'

My therapist was with a client at the time and could not get me in any earlier than my appointed 5pm, so I paced and ran and jogged while trying to calm my wild and crazy suicide notions. I kept circling back to the falls, looking over them, wondering if anyone had made the jump before. Wondering if anyone would care if I did.

Just make it to the appointment, Shannon. You can figure it out then. You don't want to do this, the voice in my head told me.

But the voice of my depression kept fighting back, telling me I DID want this.

Why wait? it said. *Why give them a chance to stop you? What do they know anyway? They don't have the same problems. They don't struggle in the same way you do. They're all overweight and out of shape and they don't care about how their lives turn out. They don't have the whole world riding on their shoulders.*

The sounds of those voices were driving me crazy. I paced the walk frantically, fighting tears so other people wouldn't be made aware of my internal struggle. I didn't want anyone to know how damaged I was, how broken and hopeless I felt. The last thing I needed was anybody's pity or sympathy. They didn't understand. And if they knew how I was feeling, they'd probably throw me back in the hospital with all the other crazy people, people I didn't belong with.

Miraculously, I made it to my appointment. When I walked into the office, my parents were there on the couch. Not a good sign. My parents are never seen together. They hate each other. Being in the same room meant I was in trouble.

I sat on the end of the couch and tried to crawl into the crack where the cushions met the back of the couch, desperate to escape the gaze of the three people who had been listening to my suicidal rant for the past few hours, who, despite their worry, seemed more upset with me. I could feel them all staring at me, wondering what to say, wondering who would break the silence first, hoping I would explain myself.

Eventually, the pressure was too much. I couldn't breathe in that room, and all I wanted was out. I stood up on the couch and leaned back to open the window to let in some air so I could breathe, not realizing what that must've looked like to three people who had been on the receiving end of my suicidal ideations for the past hour and a half. They all jumped up and yelled at me not to jump out the window. Oops!

At this point, my therapist picked up the phone and dialed 911. On me. The good girl. The valedictorian. The community service queen.

I made a bolt for the door, and my dad grabbed me, throwing me on the couch and pinning me down. And they stayed there, holding me down as I tried to claw my way out of their grip until the cops showed up.

Mortified, humiliated, face burning with shame, the cops took me from my parents and escorted me down the stairs to their cruiser. To their credit, these men looked very apologetic as they put me in the backseat, where the hard plastic of the seat jutted against the boniness of my tailbone and spine on the ride to Exeter Hospital.

I was brought into the ER and put in a waiting room with an ugly tan armchair and long beige couch that looked more like a futon from someone's dorm room than a couch that belonged in the hospital.

The nurse, a slender blonde named Candy, came to check my blood pressure and take my vitals. But this woman, despite her name, was anything but sweet. As I asked her questions about how long I would be there, when I could see my parents, if I was going to the hospital, she glared at me, telling me to shut up until the doctor got there. This woman did not know me from Adam and yet when I kept on asking questions, she exploded on me: "Why do you think your parents are even coming to see you? They deserve better than a daughter like you. You're a disgrace to your family and a lying, manipulative bitch. I won't be telling you anything. You'll just try to weasel your way out of it. You can wait here until the doctor comes to see you, whenever that may be."

At this point, I pulled away, glancing desperately around the room trying to find a place to hide. I saw that there was space under the couch, and I went for it. I got down on my hands and knees and started sliding under the couch, worming my way underneath. I couldn't see her anymore, and, from there, she couldn't hurt me. As long as I was under that couch, no one could hurt me.

And this is where I was when the doctor arrived, probably already declaring me a lunatic. And when he asked what I was doing under the couch, I told him I was protecting myself from the venom that was the ER nurse. I would not come out from under that couch until that bitch was GONE.

Candy left, and the doctor and I resumed our chat. He informed me that I would, indeed, be returning to Hampstead Hospital, but not for another few hours until they could get the paperwork through. Then he left me with my self-destructive thoughts until the men in uniform came to pick me up, strap me onto a table, and drive me to the hospital at the ungodly hour of 3AM.

Just a few hours later, at 7am, a familiar face awoke me. It was a nurse I knew from a previous trip to Hampstead Hospital. She led me out of bed and to the bathroom, where they took a sample of my urine and tested my vitals. Sleepy-eyed and hair a mess, I stumbled down the hallway, unhappy to be awake but willing to comply and do what she asked.

When I woke back up again at 8am and made my way to the front desk, I saw a couple more familiar faces greeting me. I grimaced, and they looked at me with surprise and concern. After my last visit the year before, they were sure they wouldn't be seeing me again. And yet there I was, standing in front of them, feeling every bit as fucked up as I probably had to be in order to land there again, but feeling a strange sense of security, as I knew these people, as part of their job but also as part of who they were, would accept me and receive me for exactly who I was, flaws and all.

My third, and final, stay at Hampstead Hospital was the longest, an impressive five days.

Now, obviously this is not enough time to create change. Studies have shown and self-help books proclaim that it takes 28 days to start cultivating healthy habits. It's likely that part of the reason I kept returning to the hospital was because I wasn't in rehabilitation long enough for what I was learning to sink in and become second nature.

But a large part of the halt in my recovery was due to the fact that the environment I was living in a home was not conducive to my recovery.

During this third trip to Hampstead Hospital, my psychiatrist called a family meeting, one I was hesitant to join, as the last all-family meeting I'd been at had been one giant bitch fest that pointed all fingers at me as the reason why everyone's lives sucked.

But despite my trepidation, I entered a room that contained all four of my parents seated on couches and the psychiatrist that had been assigned to me for all three of my stays.

I was delighted when the psychiatrist started to share about my accomplishments in therapy, my self-awareness, and my perseverance in recovery. I was even more thrilled when he turned his attention to my parents, saying, "I can't see how Shannon could try harder than she does, so it's my impression that perhaps the problem lies in her home environment."

FINALLY someone was calling my parents out on not doing their work to support me in recovery. Sure, they were footing the bills (no easy feat), but what really mattered: changing the way they talked to me, not criticizing me, making themselves emotionally available, listening to my plight instead of "yeah yeah yeah"ing it away - they weren't doing any of it.

And while I firmly believe now that we are the creators of our own experiences, that we are in control regardless of how others act, when you're in the midst of an eating disorder, you're functioning off a less than ideal mental operating system, one that's been hijacked by a virus called ED. Which is basically to say that until you're back in a safe place where ED isn't reigning, you need all the external support you can get to pull yourself out of that hole.

My parents never really knew what to do with me or what to say with me. In their minds, they could never win. No matter what they said, ED would find a way to twist their words to make it seem like they didn't care about me. ED was very good at that kind of mental manipulation.

Like the bitch nurse Candy, my parents were under the impression that most everything coming out of my mouth was my eating disorder speaking, not me. So when I was desperately crying out for help, they weren't believing a word I was saying. To them, they were better off safe than sorry, fearing that anything they might say or do in response to my requests would set me off on another suicidal tirade.

During this time, my twin sister, Amber, was my voice. Whether she recognized the real me underneath the voice of ED or whether she just took pity on my situation, she became the go-between between myself and my parents. She became the voice of reason when I was asking for things that would support my recovery that my parents thought was ED trying to throw me off track.

It's hard to explain even now the difference between MY voice and the voice of my eating disorder. In some ways, it's about trusting that the sufferer is really asking for help. But sometimes that doesn't work. All I can think of is that eating disorder is sabotaging your life by being mean, pushing other people away, and focusing on food, weight, and physical appearance while the person underneath is crying for help, pleading for love and support, desperate to be acknowledged as still existing beneath the eating disorder.

And help can be so many different things. It can be a hug. It can be words of reassurance. It can as simple as just listening without trying to give advice or change the other person. Just the presence of another person standing in their love for a victim of ED can be enough to crack the sufferer's heart open, like Jason did for me.

That act of cracking open the heart can radically alter the course of recovery by reminding us that we are worthy, we are deserving, and we are whole. Despite our flaws and what we have done to our bodies, we are still human and we are still here.

During that last stay at Hampstead Hospital, I was due to perform at the Allstate Chamber Music Festival. As one of the top singers in the state, it was my responsibility to learn 5 pieces of music on my own time and memorize them before the festival.

I begged my parents to allow me to perform, as garnering status as the first in the state was a huge honor. Performing in this ensemble was the culmination of all I'd worked for as a singer over the previous eight years.

The hospital gave me permission to leave for the day of Chamber, provided I return upon the conclusion of the event.

There are times when I wish I had never asked for that leave, as I can't remember a time I was more embarrassed and ashamed to perform than that day.

I arrived at the school feeling like a prisoner who had just busted loose. I had not even glanced at my sheet music, the same music I was expected to know by heart upon arrival.

The girls in my ensemble were chatty, introducing themselves to one another and sharing their rooms and scores. I recognized a few girls from other Allstate performances in years prior, but I couldn't bring myself to speak with them.

The day passed in a haze. The choir director came in, making jokes and telling us about herself and what brought her to Chamber. The pianist started up the accompaniment as I struggled to learn the music, to keep up with the girls who were supposed to be my peers. Instead, I felt alone, a total loser, unable to keep anything together.

I wanted to cry, to quit, to pack up my belongings and head back to the hospital. At least there, I was comfortable. I was among my REAL peers, and I was seen as a role model, a position I was much more comfortable with than that of the slacker who hadn't prepped for a performance.

When rehearsals came to an end, I went to the Performing Arts Center to change into my attire for the concert. Nothing fit.

I instantly flew into a frenzy, calling my parents to bring a change of clothes. "White top, black bottom," I said. They brought the clothes, but I was resistant to wearing them. I would look ridiculous. No one wanted to see me onstage, fat, bloated, and in clothes that didn't fit, my eating disorder said.

With that, I almost quit the concert. I almost threw in the towel on music, the one thing that had saved me for so long. The one thing I could lose myself in besides thoughts about food.

I ended up lip synching through the performance, feeling like a complete ass, as I knew the girls standing next to me could tell I wasn't singing. But, at that point, I didn't care. I just wanted it to be over with. I just wanted to go home and sleep and forget that day had ever happened.

That performance, or lack thereof, reminded me of everything I was losing out on through my depression and eating disorder.

But, as life often goes, things got worse, before they got better.

I was visiting my mom's house after school one day when it happened. Something about being at my mom's always set me off. It was like walking into a magnetic force field where I couldn't help but to hate myself and take it out on my body through food.

So I was over there one day when I start eating the raisins. There were plenty of other things I could've eaten, I'm sure. Maybe a loaf of bread, a granola bar in the cupboard... but food rules aren't just suggestions. They're a necessity of life. And even in recovery, I held onto those rules a little too stringently, so raisins it was.

I didn't eat sitting down. I hardly ever did when I binged. I hovered in the corner of the kitchen near the trash can with the container of raisins in hand while the other furiously shoved fistfuls into my mouth. Before I realized it, I had eaten about a quarter of the container, roughly 520 calories of sugar and carbs.

I looked at the package, utterly ashamed of myself. 'I know better than this,' I thought. 'I hope no one's watching. This is disgusting. I'm a disgusting, horrible person.'

I loathed myself and who I was in that moment. I didn't deserve to live. I didn't deserve to survive my eating disorder. I should've kept starving myself to death. That was much better than the shame and embarrassment of being a binge eater. I couldn't stand to look at myself in the mirror.

I ran upstairs to the loft and hurled myself on top of my sister's old bed. I cried and cried, berating myself, feeling so ashamed of what I'd done. I don't know how long I stayed up there. It felt like hours, but could've been only minutes.

The next thing I knew, I was in the kitchen again, to the right of the sink by trash compactor, this time with the goal of ingesting something much different, much more toxic than raisins. With trembling hands, I picked up a bottle of aspirin, unscrewed the lid, and poured them into my hand. I stared at those little white pills in the palm of my hand, filled up a glass with the metallic-tasting water from the sink, and swallowed them all.

I then walked calmly out to my car, sat down inside, and locked the doors. I pulled out my phone to text my parents and let them know what I'd done, but refused to open the doors when they came outside to get me. They threatened to call an ambulance if I wouldn't let them take me themselves. I didn't care. Not one bit. In that moment, all I wanted to do was succumb to death. I so desperately wanted to live and yet all I wanted to do was die.

Then I heard a knocking on my window. Expecting it to be my parents, I got ready to tell them off. But what I found, instead, was an elderly gentlemen standing there, knocking gently, and asking me to open the door. I rolled down the window a crack.

He told me he was a vet, a local, and that he'd heard about what I'd done. "Why would such a pretty girl like yourself want to throw your life away? Don't you have a boyfriend?" he asked. And for the life of me, I couldn't answer him. I had everything going for me: valedictorian of my class, one of the top singers in the state, guaranteed acceptance to any college I wanted to go to. Yet all I knew was that death was a much preferable option to the pain and suffering I felt inside all the time.

And I'll tell you what: To this day, we still have no idea who in the hell that man was, where he came from, or how he had heard about me. All we know is that the universe sent me a very kind, open-hearted guardian angel to stay with me while we waited for the ambulance to arrive.

When it did arrive, we found that a close family friend was the paramedic on call and a couple of my parents' friends from the fire department had arrived as well. I felt humiliated as this man and his female co-worker lifted me into the ambulance in front of all these people who knew me, but didn't really know the half of what I was struggling with and how it affected my family.

Once in the ambulance, I called my buddy Jason, my human life line, and said, "J, I did something stupid. I'm so sorry," and proceeded to let him know what had happened and that I wouldn't be able to make it to our outing the next day.

The female EMT cut my call short to tell me that I'd have to have my stomach pumped, explaining to me the process they'd use. I refused. No way in hell was I putting charcoal and shit in my body. "What if I don't want to?" I asked. "Then we'll force it into you," was her response. I'm sure she made a lot of friends with that attitude.

The details after that are hazy. We arrived at the hospital. They put me in a gown and had me sit in a waiting room forever. My parents showed up, worried and nervous. And they didn't end up pumping my stomach after all.

In fact, they didn't do much of anything. Considering that this was the first time I'd ever done something that very well could have killed me, they were pretty lenient about the whole thing.

They sent me home instead of to the psych ward, where they had sent me the past three times I had attempted or contemplated suicide. I slept off the drug-induced haze, and we pretended like it had never happened. (My family's good at that.)

Later that month, after my release from the hospital, I was due to perform Carl Orff's "Carmina Burana" with a select group of high school singers alongside the college singers at the University of New Hampshire.

Carmina Burana was a breeze for me, as I'd memorized it for a major performance with my choir my freshmen year of high school. Going back to UNH to perform was an incredible experience, as I had participated in their Summer Youth Music School years before and visited with my Select Choir for their Clark-Terry Jazz Music Festival. The campus was a familiar sight and flooded me with warm memories.

After spending the day practicing with the choir and orchestra, we broke for dinner. I ate a protein bar I had brought in the empty choir room, content to continue running through the numbers until everyone else came back from the dining hall.

Then hunger rumbled in my stomach, forcing me to pay attention. I acted without thinking, pulling a five from my purse and heading to the vending machine to find something vegan and healthy that I could buy to feed myself.

I scarfed down the bag of nuts that popped out of the vending machine door. That's when the anxiety settled in.

You're going to get fat! my eating disorder told me. *How could you do this to us? You're a pig! Who does that? Who goes to a vending machine and actually BUYS something?! I can't believe you ate that!*

I was freaking out. I didn't know what to do. Before I was aware of what was happening, I had my mood stabilizing medication in hand and was swallowing the pills with gulp after gulp of water.

Then it hit me: Oh shit. I did it again.

I picked up my cell and dialed my best friend, Micaela.

"Micaela," I said when she picked up the phone, "I did something stupid."

And I told her what had happened.

She call in her mom, and together they researched the impact taking all those pills would have.

There aren't words to describe what those moments were like. Crying, waiting to hear the prognosis for my life. Knowing that I couldn't take back my actions and there was a chance I would pay the ultimate price for my mistake: death. Realizing that despite my actions, I didn't *want* to die; I just felt like there was no other choice. In my head, it was either follow the rules or DIE. Getting fat, to me, felt like the end. The thought of getting fat felt like my life was over.

Fortunately, the pills had no other effect than making me tired and a bit nauseous.

I skipped the concert in favor of crying in the chorus room, never telling anyone that I hadn't actually been a part of the performance (surprise, Mr Harrington!).

After the raisin ordeal and the Carmina scare, the psychiatrist changed my medication, convinced that a new medicine with a stronger dosage was exactly what I needed to keep my shit together.

As it would turn out, all the medication got me was a car accident and a couple late papers, due to some of the side effects I wasn't warned about, including dizziness, difficulty concentrating, and fatigue.

One day after school, I met with my dad at the park for a walk. As we traversed a path through the woods and alongside a stream, I asked my dad to take a leap of faith with me.

"Dad," I said, "I can't live like this. I feel like a zombie. I can't focus. I can't concentrate. This isn't life, because I'm not really LIVING it. I want to propose something, a trial period of sorts. Give me 3 months off the medicine. I'll do the work with Jason. I'll talk to the therapist. Just give me 3 months. If I can't get myself together, if I can't beat this, if I try to hurt myself again, you can put me back on the meds. But, please, I'm begging you: Let me try this on my own."

And I can't even begin to imagine what that must have been like for my dad, to struggle with the choice between keeping his daughter safe and giving her back her life. But in the end, he opted to let me try things on my own.

The combination of getting off meds, the fear I'd experienced in the moments between trying to take my life and fearing that I may have done myself in, and the deep inner knowing that I was here to *do something*, not throw my life away, brought about the change that was needed.

The next few months flew by in a flurry as I threw myself into activities that I could put my heart and soul into.

I began working every day after school at the Organic Garden Cafe, the same restaurant Jason was the manager of. The smiling people, the caring coworkers, and the high vibing energy of the place lifted my spirits even on the darkest of days. I couldn't get enough of it. I showed up whenever I had time to spare and could make the 45-minute drive over.

I started out washing dishes. Then the prep started asking me for help in preparing some of the dishes during the busy dinner hour. Then I started stepping in for the barista while she was on break or if someone didn't show up for their shift. Before long, I was waitressing. The constant acquiring of new skills kept my mind busy and the Organic Garden, or the OG as we called it, became my safe haven from negativity. I finally felt like I belonged somewhere, like I was surrounded by people who understood and embraced me.

One night, when I was closing up, I noticed a group of teenagers through the window of the pizza parlor next door. My heart contracted as I realized that I did not have a group of friends like that, although I wished I did. While other kids my age were out enjoying pizza and the company of their friends on a Friday night, I was closing down a restaurant alone, my coworkers having left earlier at my behest, as I preferred the quiet of the restaurant at night. Loneliness and loss hit me like a punch in the gut. Would I ever have friends like that? Would I ever have those kinds of experiences?

I spent my entire eating disorder pushing other people away, afraid to let people get close and discover how flawed I truly was. I didn't want others to see my struggle, and I didn't believe that they could help me. I was so used to taking care of myself. From a young age, I was taught to depend on myself, to be self-reliant. *I don't* need *anyone else,* I thought. And I used that to justify my isolation. But, ultimately, eating disorders thrive on isolation, and it wasn't until I began connecting with others again, like Jason and my coworkers at the OG, that my future started looking a little brighter.

I also spent a lot of time in the woods, getting lost and finding my way back to the trailhead. Being in nature helped to give me perspective. The expansiveness of it brought me back to how much more there is to life than just the narrative that kept playing in my head.

My parents also assigned me to a new therapist, one who was closer to school. I would visit her office once a week.

The first time we met, once I was settled on the couch, she looked me straight in the eye and asked point blank, "Does it bother you that I'm fat?" The question unsettled me. I hadn't thought about it that way. My eating disorder was not about being thin. It was about being *good*, being *right*, being *better* so that maybe I would be good enough for those around me. I didn't once stop to think that by thinking this, I was condemning those who were overweight.

So I told the therapist, "No, it doesn't bother me," and we commenced our short-lived therapy arrangement. I showed up at her office, she would lead me through a guided imagery exercise that often put me to sleep, and it would forever go down in my memory as a glorified nap time.

While I'd like to say that this period was all kittens and rainbows and easy recovery, the truth is that just as I had fallen into anorexia and bulimia, I dove headfirst into binges.

One sunny afternoon on my way home from school, I found myself in a panic. What about, I couldn't tell you. But I found myself pulling into the drive-thru of a Taco Bell and KFC in Haverhill, one town over from my school, the city I was raised in. Being vegan, I could only order certain things off the menu, so I ordered potato wedges from the KFC drive-thru, then pulled up to the window of the Taco Bell to order bean burritos without the cheese.

I ate the potatoes and burritos with voracity as I pulled onto the highway, worried that someone might see me through the windows. I was about to embark on what would go down as my most epic binge. I felt terrible, horrible, awful, fat. I felt out of control, and I was convinced that I was an awful person. Why was this happening to me? Thoughts about my lack of willpower and self-control filled my head, causing my drive to fly by, the time entirely lost to these frantic self-judgments.

When I signaled right off the exit to get home, without thinking, I pulled a u-ie (u-turn) right into the parking lot of a Dunkin' Donuts, where I ordered a plain bagel. I crammed it down my throat as I navigated the backroads to my favorite small natural foods store, the Natural Grocer. There, I picked up my favorite hummus and veggie wrap.

I can't believe I'm doing this, I thought. *What's wrong with me? This is such a waste of money! I'm going to get so fat! I can't believe I'm spending money to make myself fat. I'm such an idiot. No wonder no one loves me. No wonder no one likes me or wants to be friends with me. How could they?*

As I wolfed down the wrap, my car steered itself to the Tannery, a shopping complex in Newburyport, close to my parents' house. I walked into the bakery there and ordered a huge muffin they had made that morning. I sheepishly paid for my order, convinced that they knew exactly what was going on. That they knew that I'd already had a day's worth of food in the previous thirty minutes of my drive home. I thought they'd say something, stop me from making my purchase. But they sold me the muffin and let me go on my way. That muffin did not come apart crumb by crumb. No; I bit off such huge chunks of that muffin I practically choked on it.

When I got home, I found myself in front of the freezer, staring at a frozen chocolate cake that Steppy had left over from someone's birthday. I had been slicing off slivers of the cake in the previous weeks, allowing myself to enjoy a food I had avoided entirely while I was anorexic. But in the mode I was in, I just grabbed the rest of the cake, a fork, and dug in. All I could think of was how guilty I felt. This wasn't my cake. Steppy was going to come home and want some of the cake, and it would be gone. I'd be disappointing her, and my dad, *again*. I was a horrible child, an awful kid. In that moment, I truly thought they'd be better off without me.

So many of my binges felt like that: out of control, completely dissociated, and guilt-ridden. I thought in those moments that everyone could see right through me. They could see how impulsive I was, how disgusting I was. They could see the invisible crumbs on my face. They could see the food sitting like a rock in my stomach. While the binge eating was making me more solid, more fleshed out, all I felt was transparent; and that was the scariest thing of all. For a lifetime, I had become accustomed to being noticed: awards for community service, dancing on stage, as an accoladed singer; but what I wasn't used to was being *seen*, not for my accomplishments, but as a human being. That feeling of transparency brought about feelings of great shame, because I wasn't sure that what people were seeing was any good, if it was as screwed up to them as I felt.

That wasn't the only time I binged on my drive home.

I often found myself eating in the car, the only place I felt like I was truly alone, away from everyone else. Even if I was in a parking lot or the driveway or parked on the side of the road, it was like no one could see through the metal that encased me, despite the very obvious fact that I had clear glass windows on my 4-door sedan.

One of my favorite binge food combinations was Medjool dates and avocados. To most people, this doesn't really sound like a binge food. In fact, it sounds pretty healthy! But, to me, dates and avocados were two of the highest calorie raw foods I could eat. They were my kryptonite. The creaminess of an avocado and the sweetness of a date couldn't be matched by any other raw food, although there were several others I'd fallen in love with. Because I deprived myself of these foods, justifying it by calorie count, these forbidden foods made the perfect choice for a binge.   I would sit outside the Natural Grocer with a bag of dates and two avocados, mowing those babies down like they were going out of style.

I confided in my dad that dates were my weakness, and we came up with what we thought would be a good incentive for ending the binge eating, especially where trigger foods like dates, sushi, and muffins were concerned.

The plan was that for every time I binged on those foods, I would pay my dad $50. Well, that happened a couple of times before we realized that $50 wasn't doing the trick. So we upped the ante to $100 per binge. Yet I kept on eating and eating and overeating. We finally came to the conclusion that money wasn't a strong motivator for me, and that the eating disorder was much stronger than any kind of monetary incentive or punishment.

If I were to describe the compulsion to eat, it would be like talking about the force between two magnets. Food called to me like a ghost in the night. It took a while before I even realized that I was bingeing. I would be lying in bed, stomach round and swollen from stuffing myself past the point of being full, when it would hit me, "Oh my God. I just binged." Over time, the awareness of a binge crept forward - bingeing and realizing it, but continuing the binge; binging and realizing it, then making the seriously concerted effort to stop (usually by taking a nap until the urge went away); starting a binge, then putting the food down; recognizing the oncoming binge and walking away from it.

My worst memories of bingeing were of hiding it.

Because I was committed to doing the 80/10/10 lifestyle, it wasn't considered part of my diet to eat the kind of gourmet raw food we served at the Organic Garden. But as a prep and a server, I often got to sample the dishes before they went on the menu.

The food was delicious, but I always felt guilty, like Jason would find out that I was eating these gourmet raw foods and be disappointed in me for not sticking with just fruits and leafy greens. I don't know why I thought I had to hide it from him. He was the most loving and forgiving person I'd ever met, and that's probably why I was afraid more than anything to let him down.

So I would wait until Jason wasn't looking to eat the food. I would pretend that the dish on the rack where we hung our jackets belonged to someone else. I would pop a raw ravioli in my mouth when he left the kitchen to head to the front of the house to speak with a customer. I would sneak foods when I went to the basement to restock - a cacao chip cookie here, a slice of raw rye bread there.

In addition to hiding my eating from Jason, I was hiding it from my coworkers as well. I didn't want them to see how much I was eating. I was already the biggest female employee they had. I didn't want them to see that it was because I couldn't stop myself. Because every time I went to the basement kitchen, I was grabbing soaked apricots or sun dried tomatoes to munch on. Because I ate every plate that got messed up or was extra when an order was canceled. I became paranoid that there were cameras in the building, that all of the food I was sneaking would be found out, and I'd get into big trouble.

I justified taking the food because I had spent dozens, maybe even hundreds, of hours volunteering before I became part of the paid staff at the OG. As part of the volunteer arrangement, I was allowed free meals and smoothies according to the number of hours I'd spent volunteering. But because I had never logged my hours, I didn't have an accurate record of how much food I was "owed", and I certainly didn't want to document the process of what I had "bought" in exchange for that time, as I knew that Jason would see those logs. Jason represented the best part of me, and I couldn't bear to have him see the choices I was making about what to eat.

Sometimes, once we had closed down the register for the evening, I would look in the display case at the baked goods, salivating with desire to snatch up one of those scrumptious treats. I'd end up grabbing one, then putting the money for it along with a note in the cash register, pretending that someone else had bought it after we'd closed.

All of this hiding took its toll on me. I was constantly fearful that people would figure out how much I was eating. I pulled up the trash to hide my wrappers under everything else, then offered to take out the trash myself so no one would see them when they were dumping out the bin. It took a lot of mental effort to keep people from finding me out, although they could tell by the weight I was rapidly gaining, the pounds that were accumulating on my body after months of starvation. Somehow, though, if I kept that part under wraps, then maybe I wasn't as fucked up as I thought I was. I mean, who goes from anorexia and bulimia to binge eating? I had to hide how different I was to keep others from thinking even less of me than I was sure they already did.

Spring 2010 - Finding Balance & Recovery

That spring, I was named a Horatio Alger Scholar, a scholarship based on a combination of community service and involvement, academic achievement, and the overcoming of adversity.

In addition to being given a $20,000 scholarship for college, Horatio Alger scholars were also given an all expenses paid trip to Washington D.C.

Trouble was it took place on the same weekend as my All State concert. And if I didn't go on the trip, the scholarship was void.

With a heavy heart, I spoke with my choir director to give him the news that I would not be going to All State. He looked at me like I was crazy. "Shannon, you've got the opportunity to get $20,000 to go to college AND they're sending you to D.C. Of course I wouldn't expect you to go to All State!" But despite his statement, I couldn't help but feel like I was letting him, and my choir, down by not representing us at that final concert.

In April, I flew down to D.C. to join the 100 or so other scholars for a few days of who knew what. We were put up in a beautiful hotel -

second only to the Ritz Carlton. My roommate, as I would come to find out, was bulimic, which was why we were roomed together. But despite our common ground having eating disorders, we didn't really hit it off.

Over the week, I met a number of really amazing young adults, many of whom had been through trauma much more significant than mine: growing up homeless, parents murdered, orphaned, parents who were addicted to drugs... Again, I felt like I did not belong. *My problems aren't nearly this bad,* I thought. *I don't deserve to be here. Someone else should be here.*

Some people look at an eating disorder as a huge problem, something they could never begin to comprehend. Even now, people tell me, "It must've been horrible. I'm so sorry you had to go through that." But after a while, it just became part of life. The thoughts started to seem like my own. In a way, they became comfortable, since I was so used to thinking them. So amongst a group of my peers, other young people who had handled some of life's more difficult experiences early on, I still felt out of place.

Before my arrival, I had informed the hosts that I was on a raw vegan diet. The hotel did a beautiful job creating elaborate plates of vegetables, pates, and fruits to meet my dietary requirements. But when no one was looking during breaks, I would grab cookies off the tray on the snack table, devouring several on a trip to the "bathroom" so that no one would see me eating them.

I felt so guilty. My heart raced while I ate those cookies, wiping the crumbs off my shirt to rid myself of the evidence, my hand aggressively swiping at my mouth to make sure there was nothing there. *You fat pig*, the voice in my head said, *I can't believe you. Those aren't even vegan! Do you know how bad cookies are for you? Do you know how fat you're going to get? God, look at you. You're already huge. You had to buy all new skirts for this trip. Do you really want to buy more another size up when you get home? You disgust me.*

Those thoughts were the reason the trip went by in a blur and why I hardly remember most of my teenage years, as they were so wrapped up in self-judgment and thoughts about food, weight, and my body that I was too busy to notice, much less recall, anything else.

In addition to the neverending internal dialogue about food, I experienced terrible bouts of insomnia, often not falling asleep until 2 or 3 in the morning, when my alarm was set to wake me up bright and early at 6 to prepare for my day and a 45-minute drive to school. I spent fitful, sleepless nights in bed trying desperately to close my eyes and get some sleep, never being able to escape the nightmare of my day-to-day reality.

The psychiatrist, upon hearing of my sleep troubles, issued me a heavy dose of sleeping pills. He told me to take one whenever I had trouble falling asleep.

At this point, I was so wrapped up in holistic health, eschewing conventional medicine, that I didn't want to take the drug. I knew that there was a reason I wasn't sleeping, I just couldn't figure out what it was, which was driving me crazy. (Seriously, all of those sleepless nights were starting to take their toll).

During this struggle with insomnia, I had the craziest adventures while trying to put myself to sleep.

Sometimes I would get hungry in the night, but I didn't have anything in the house that I could, or would, eat. And, of course, in the wee hours of the morning, the only thing that's open is Taco Bell and gas stations. Other than that, there's not much in terms of options or variety, especially when you're trying to be health conscious and eat mostly raw food.

This led me to the Shell station in town that was open 24/7. Amidst the racks and racks of chemically processed, preservative-added, artificially-dyed crap, I found something I could eat: Bananas. Which sounds ridiculous, I know, to get up in the middle of the night and drive 6 miles just for a banana or two, but there was something comforting about being able to get what I wanted regardless of the time of day (or night).

On another restless night, I made my way over to the beach. Now, spring-time at the beach in New England, especially in the dead of the night, is by no means warm and cozy. But a part of my screwed up brain thought that maybe it was being in the house, in the energy that had built up from arguments, bingeing, and self-destruction, that was keeping me awake. Maybe the waves with their gentle rise and fall, crashing on the beach in a soothing lullaby, would lull me to sleep. No such luck. Instead, I spent hours on the beach, eyes wide open, shivering against the cold sand and wondering why in the heck I had thought this would be a good idea. Despite the cold and the wind that blew sand into my eyes, nose, and mouth, I found myself unwilling to leave and return home. If only I could sleep, then, perhaps, things would be better. Then maybe I'd find some peace…

One evening, after I had spent hours surfing the internet and reading a book, trying desperately to fall asleep and dream, I caved.

I grabbed the handwritten prescription from the doctor, pulled on a coat, and took off for the 24-hour pharmacy at the CVS in town. I didn't want to take those pills. I didn't even know if they'd work. Hell, it was so early in the morning that it would probably knock me out for the entire day, but I didn't care.

After depositing my prescription, I realized I had left my wallet in the car. It was locked. On the seat, staring at me, were my keys and cell phone. *Motherfucker.* Only someone as stupid as myself would venture out alone this time of night then lock her keys in the car. What an idiot.

I was at a loss for what to do. Should I just sit and wait? Should I start walking back to the island? There was hardly anyone awake at this hour.

That's when I noticed the cop car.

I stood next to the vehicle, hoping that its owner would come out soon and help me. I wasn't waiting for long when an officer in uniform walked out of the convenience store on the corner, sandwich and potato chips in hand.

He looked at me, perplexed as to why I was standing next to his vehicle.

"Ummm… sir?" I asked tentatively. "I've locked my keys in the car. I live on the island. Is there any way you could drive me home so I could pick up my spare set?"

The cop, bless his heart, agreed. As we drove down the turnpike to Plum Island, the cop offered me some of his chips. I declined, pitying the poor man for having to eat chips and a sandwich because of the lack of good food available for those working the overnight shift.

At the house, I fumbled around in the dark, reaching under the grill for the camouflaged magnetic key set my Dad kept hanging there in case one of us should arrive at home without our keys.

Once inside, I crept to my room, located my spare key, and headed back out to the cop car.

We headed back to town, where I picked up my prescription and bid the cop adieu. When I got home, I took the pills, falling asleep in no time, waking up halfway through the next day. Having missed most of school, I decide to just take the day off and, as I usually did when I didn't feel like going to school, asked me doctor to write me a note to have my absence excused. She obliged without question, knowing that if I said I needed time off, I probably did. It was nice to have someone, at least, who understood that I was trying to take care of myself as best I could.

My senior year of high school was coming to a close, and tickets for prom were on sale. While I never would've guessed growing up that I'd skip my prom, I just couldn't bring myself to go. I felt so far removed from my classmates, like I had been on a whole separate journey while they had been building memories and lifelong friendships, that going to prom felt like rubbing salt in an open wound. Who would I dance with? Who would I take as my date?

My coworker at the OG, Joe, offered to come with me, as he had missed his own high school prom. Of course, I also considered asking Jason. But both requests for guests were declined, as both were over the age of 21 and thus were liable to bring alcohol to underage kids.

So, with that, I decided to skip prom. While everyone else, including my tomboyish sister, fussed over dresses and shoes, I just kept working away at the OG, learning the ropes and picking up any shifts I could - not for the money, but for the escape.

On the day of prom, I was scheduled to work my usual Friday night closing shift. Seniors were dismissed early to prepare for the evening's festivities, so I found myself with some time before work. As I drove home, it hit me: No matter how much I hated school, no matter how few friends I had, I couldn't miss my own prom. I was certain, in that moment, that I'd regret it if I did.

I called my sister, who called the school's principal and police officer to arrange my late registration for the event. "You'll miss the promenade," they said, "And you won't be able to come for the dinner. Just the dancing." That was all fine by me. I had no one to walk with anyway, and I wasn't going to be able to eat anything off the buffet, either.

I drove home, rifled through my closet, and found a black cocktail dress I had bought on clearance just a few months before but never worn. I picked out two sets of jewelry and shoes, then packed it all up into the car and headed over to Amber's friend Noelle's house, where everyone else was getting ready.

After lacing up dresses and taking dozens of photos on the lawn, Amber, her friends, and their dates loaded into the limo, while I hung back with the parents. That was when I started questioning my choice: *Should I really do this? What will everyone think? I've already told everyone I'm not going, and now I'm just going to show up, unannounced, right before the dancing? God, this is going to be so embarrassing. I don't have a proper dress or a date!* I idled, chatting with my parents and my grandmother, until the clock finally told me it was time to head to the country club where they were hosting our prom.

My heart raced with anticipation as I parked my car and walked up the walkway towards the front doors of the building. I became more and more self-conscious with every step. *I look fat in this dress. Why did I even decide to do this? It's not like anyone here is going to care whether I show up or not. And who wears black to prom anyway? I'm so stupid.*

I bumped into Officer Marsilia, our school's police officer, at the door and she let me in. As I walked down the steps to the ballroom, I saw my best friend Micaela sitting at the table directly in front of the door. Her back was to me, but someone must have told her I showed up, because she stood up and ran to the door to give me a big hug. I could've cried. Micaela, at least, was happy that I'd shown up, and that was enough for me.

I sat down at the table and chatted with everyone while they finished eating; then we hit the dance floor. I had a blast. For a time, I even forgot about how fat I looked and felt. I was even grateful for the cocktail dress, as its short skirt allowed me to stay cool and keep dancing while everyone else ducked outside to cool off in their long, heavy gowns.

There are so many memories and experiences I have forsaken because of my eating disorder. Prom may not have been one of my top ten memories, but I am grateful that I at least had one normal high school experience, if you can call it that, to look back on.

Pretty soon, it was time for graduation. As valedictorian of our class, I was slated to stand up at the podium and give a speech. For probably the first time in my life - my friends and family know me as the chatty and talkative type - I was at a loss for what to say. How could I communicate to these kids, my peers, all that I'd been experiencing and learning? Because while the previous months may not have seemed to be all that special, they were full of some pretty potent healing and powerful lessons, enough so that I finally felt confident that I would recover.

I researched other speeches online and listened to some of the most memorable speeches, ones that went down in school history or were seen millions of times on YouTube. Eventually, I crafted a speech that I hoped would contain some humor and some inspiration for my fellow students. In it, I included my favorite quote: "Change the way you look at things, and the things you look at change." This quote summarized all that I'd been learning from self-help books and my time with Jason. Life isn't what happens to you; it's what you make of it.

By the time graduation rolled around, I had disenrolled from my college of choice (Champlain College in Burlington, VT), partially because they didn't offer me a full tuition scholarship and partially because I wasn't even sure what I wanted to do at that point. I felt that going to college just because it was the "next step" didn't really suit me.

Instead, I found myself online late one night, searching for career opportunities in the field of holistic health. That's when I stumbled upon the Institute for Integrative Nutrition and the opportunity to become a health coach. The teachers were some of the same people whose books I had been reading for the past year or so, and the description matched what I wanted to offer so perfectly. Because I was under 18 and didn't have a credit card to sign up, I had my dad enroll me the next day, and I wrote him a check for the tuition from my savings account.

Not quite two months after graduation, before the Integrative Nutrition course started online, my dad approached me to talk. "Hey kiddo, so you're not going to school around here, right?" "Nope. The school is all online, so I can do it from anywhere." "Have you considered moving?"

While this conversation is humorous in retrospect, my dad kicking me out in the form of a question and answer, it felt like a punch to the gut. Here I was, just about to start school, feeling pretty stable in my recovery, having absolutely no idea what I was going to do with my life other than study to become a health coach, and my dad is, yet again, giving me the boot.

I talked about moving to California, because it seemed like a pretty cool place to live. Finally, my mom convinced me to move to Florida - across the country, but in a southerly direction, and I had family there, in case times got tough. I called my grandparents and spoke with them about moving down there and living with them until I was 18 and could get a place of my own. I had already booked tickets to visit them in October, so we decided I'd just move down then.

When my dad got wind of the plan to move to Florida, he asked me another question: "Aren't you going down to visit in October?" "Yeah," I said, "That's when I'm planning on moving down." After that, he called my grandparents and negotiated to have me fly down in August - just two weeks after our conversation about moving out.

As I usually did when traveling, I packed my bags the day I bought the tickets - or, in this case, changed my roundtrip flight into a one-way trip - and I basically sat on my luggage until my flight left for Florida.

My dad promised to drive down my car and the rest of my belongings shortly after my arrival.

While I was excited to move, excited to be free and explore the world on my own, I also felt rushed to say goodbyes. With so few days before my departure, I didn't have a chance to spend quality time with everyone I had to say goodbye to. So when I left for Florida, it was with a heart full of hope for a better quality of life and a sadness for all the unfinished relationships I was leaving behind.

Fall 2010-Today - Freedom

Moving to Florida and being away from most of my family was the linchpin of my recovery. Being removed from the daily triggers disguised as interactions with my parents gave me the mental and emotional capacity to start exploring what my eating disorder was about. It allowed me to pay more attention to my thoughts and where they were coming from.

Over the next several years, my travels and studies brought my eating disorder to a close and found me in an emotional space in which I could finally be OK around food and comfortable in my body. There were many people, institutions, organizations, schools of thought, workshops, classes, and experiences that taught me during that time. Just as an eating disorder is not caused by any one thing, recovery cannot be limited to just one lesson or type of therapy. There are so many options for healing your body, mind, and spirit.

One of the biggest lessons I learned in my recovery is about the power of thoughts and perception. Nothing has meaning except the meaning we give it. It's not what is happening or what happened to me that's important; it's how I view that experience. Am I making it a bad thing? Am I making myself a victim of circumstances? Or am I finding the lesson in the difficulties and moving forward?

Taking control of my thoughts and learning how to shift my perception of my experience played a critical role in allowing me to release the past and live the happy, extraordinary life I do today.

Now, my life is very different from what it was during my eating disorder. I have an abundance of friends, an active social life, and a career I love: helping other women learn how to love themselves, their bodies, and their life. The eating disorder that was supposed to be my undoing was the inception of the life I live today.

In certain moments, such as when I'm driving down the highway on a hot summer day, windows down, music blaring, or when I'm greeting my friends' new baby in the hospital, I am overwhelmed with gratitude, and joy floods my body, reminding me that *I am here*. I exist, and I am worthy - of love, of friendship, and of recovery. These are the moments I live for - the ones that bring me back to reality and all that is. And for that I couldn't be more grateful.

Afterword

I know that some people will come to me once this book is written asking, "Well, what about recovery?" This book was written with the intention of helping people to understand what it's like to have an eating disorder, to give them a glimpse into the minds of anorexia, bulimia, binge eating disorder, and even depression. But this book was never intended to be a manual for recovery. That subject itself is a whole 'nother book, perhaps one I will take on writing in the future.

The best advice I can give to those in recovery is this: Keep going. You will always make it through as long as you keep putting one foot in front of the other. You may fall off track at times. You may stumble. You may backtrack a bit. That's all OK. Just keep pressing ahead. You are never in the same spot twice. When you find yourself backtracking, you will discover that you now have new insights, tools, and resources for how to deal with this situation, rather than allow yourself to succumb to the downward spiral you've become accustomed to when the voice of your eating disorder pipes back up.

Also, reach out for support, but not just any support. Find the support that works for YOU. Eating disorder support groups work for some and not for others. There are all kinds of therapies and types of psychology. Figure out what resonates with you, rather than settling for the first one you find or the one your insurance covers. Getting the right support is crucial in recovery.

For those who have a loved one who is suffering with an eating disorder, the best I can offer you is this: Love them unconditionally. An eating disorder is a form of protection - protection from pain, from being hurt, from facing fears. Instead of judging the eating disorder as bad, seek to understand the service that it's offering and to find a way in which you can fill that need that doesn't result in self-destruction.

Recovery takes time. It takes patience. It will not happen on your timeline. If your loved one slips up, don't get upset. Recognize that this, too, is part of the process, and embrace it. Offer your unconditional love, support, and acceptance throughout the entire process.

And for God's sake, stop trying to change people. As much as we may want someone to recover, it's not our job nor our responsibility to make them do anything. They have to make the choice for themselves. Do your best to inspire those you love to continue to choose life over death and love over fear.

This is what has created lasting change - for myself as well as those I know who are recovered. May it be a support to you and those you love in your journeys.

Acknowledgments

No book is a one woman project.

Of course, this book never would've been written if it wasn't for the support, love, and encouragement from my fans, readers, and clients. Thank you. Thank you for blessing my life and giving me the opportunity to share what I've learned with you day in and day out. You are phenomenal.

And to the folks who quite literally saved my life: Micaela Russell, Deanna Pappas, and Jason Long. Without you lifting me up, I wouldn't be around to write this. Same goes for my peeps at the Organic Garden – your vibrant energy was my salvation.

Jason and Micaela, I owe you both a special thanks. Jason, for being my teacher and life preserver. Micaela, for being my rock, my hand to hold, my sister, and my best friend. Every time I write my story, every time I share my life experience, I am overcome with a huge debt of gratitude to you for saving my life. I truly would not the person I am today, would likely not be alive today, if it was not for your love and friendship. Thank you for being my inspiration, my will to live, and my mentors during undoubtedly the most dark and difficult time in my life. <3

All the love in the world goes out to my family, who, through hell and high water, stood behind me, even when they didn't know what the heck I was doing or why I was doing it. Thanks for believing in me. <3

Love and thanks to my first love, Jesse Abercrombie, who supported me through the tail end of my eating disorder and sought to understand me, frustrating as it was at times. And who also generously proofed the book, knowing how important it is to me that this book be of the highest quality possible. Thank you for taking good care of this book and giving of your time, love, and heart to see it through to completion.

HUGE HUGE HUGE love, gratitude, and mad respect to Chase Boehringer, my personal cheerleader and ass kicker through the whole process of making this book a reality.

Massive doses of love & gratitude to my coach, Danielle Rondeau, whose wisdom, insightful questioning, and fierce love helped me get through the book-writing process.

Hugs & kisses to my amazing clients, who have taught me just how powerful food freedom really is - not just in theory, but in practice.

Thanks to the folks at Hampstead Hospital for taking such good care of me, and a BIG hug and thank you to Monika Ostroff, Rhys Wyman, and Dr. Stacy Sheehan for their TLC and never-ending support throughout my recovery.

Gratitude and appreciation goes to The Institute for Integrative Nutrition, for helping me heal, teaching me to coach, and allowing me to have the career of my dreams, to the Option Institute, for allowing me to break through the limitations I'd created for myself in my mind, and to the wonderful light beings Omega Institute, for helping me come out of my shell. Also, specifically to Lindsey Smith and Joshua Rosenthal for really pushing me to get this book out there and out of my head.

Big love to my friends at Charlotte Street Pub for letting me show up every night to sit in the back corner and write, basket of fries and hot toddy at the ready. And to the folks at High Five Coffee Bar for allowing me to sit at the corner table 'til my foot fell asleep writing chapter after chapter. You guys rock. BIG HUGS to Michael Trufant, the talented and generous videographer who put together the promo for "Why Can't You Just Eat?"

And a shout out to all the other amazing teachers I've gotten to share my life with thus far: Rick Gabrielly, Marcus Ambrester, Naomi Paulson Calderon, Tom Kendall, Tom Lake, Lisa Lake, Kenny Button, Scott Houston, Ali Smith, Andy Gonzalez, Atman Smith, Dan Millman, Beverly Haberman, Clyde Haberman, Barry Neil Kaufman, Raun Kaufman, Stan Cohen, Christian Hollingsworth, Jordan Ambrester, Tristan Ambrester, Jackie Lieske, Brett Bevell, Hailey Vincent, Lauren Medeiros, Jason Collins, Erin Swift, Sophia Georgia, Lauren Amerson, DahVid Weiss, Amanda Ratkowski, Rochelle Hudson, Katie Cleary, Andrew Snow, David Donoghue, Michelle Zambuto, Rachel Feldman, and so many more, it would be impossible to name them all.

The deepest depths of my heart cannot express the insane amount of gratitude I have for you all. Thank you.

Last, but certainly not least, this book goes to Lucy Alexander. If there's an angel in heaven looking out for me, I am certain it's you. Thank you for sharing with me your strength, your love, and your encouragement.

Resources

These are some people and resources I have found inspiring and useful in my own recovery. I hope they bring you the hope and healing they have brought to my own life.

Academy for Eating Disorders - www.aedweb.org
Alissa Sulli - http://www.alyssasulli.com/break-free-program.html
Beating Binge Eating - http://beatingbingeeating.com/
Body Confidence - www.alisonleipzig.com
Chelsey Benzel - http://www.chelseybwellness.com/
Cheryl Richardson - www.cherylrichardson.com
Christie Inge - www.christieinge.com
Crazy Wild Love Academy - www.alexismeads.com
Eat Q - www.eatq.com
Eat Sanely - www.eatsanely.com
Eating Disorder Hope - www.eatingdisorderhope.com
Eating Mindfully - www.eatingmindfully.com
Eliza Ceci - www.peaceonmyplate.com
Elizabeth Mauro - www.elizabethmauro.com
Ellie Savoy - www.dietfreeandhealthy.com
Emily Rosen - www.emilyjoyrosen.com
Emotional Eating Support Group -
www.facebook./groups/endingemotionaleating
Girls on the Run - www.girlsontherun.org
HungerforHappiness.com - www.HungerforHappiness.com
Hungry for Happiness - www.samanthaskelly.com
Institute for Integrative Nutrition - www.integrativenutrition.com
Institute for the Psychology of Eating - www.psychologyofeating.com

The International Association of Eating Disorders Professionals Foundation - www.iaedp.com

Intuitive Eating- www.intuitiveating.com

Isabel Foxen Duke - www.isabelfoxenduke.com

Jason Garner - www.jasongarner.com

Jenni Schaefer - www.jennischaefer.com

Jess Weiner - www.jessweiner.com

Jon Gabriel - www.thegabrielmethod.com

Live More Weigh Less - www.sarahjenks.com

Louise Hay - www.louisehay.com

Mara Glatzel - www.maraglatzel.com

Mark Manson - www.markmanson.com

Michelle May - www.amihungry.com

Mike Hrotoski - www.mikehrotoski.com

More to Love - www.moretolovewithrachel.com

National Association of Anorexia Nervosa - www.anad.org

National Eating Disorders Association (NEDA) - www.nationaleatingdisorders.org

The Omega Institute for Holistic Studies - www.eomega.org

The Option Institute - www.option.org

Pleasurable Weight Loss - www.jenalaflamme.com

Project Heal - www.projectheal.org

Psych Central - www.psychcentral.com

Recovery from Food Addiction - http://kaysheppard.com/

The Representation Project - www.therepresentationproject.org

Rob Scott - www.robscott.com

Shrink Yourself - www.shrinkyourself.com

T.H.E. Center for Disordered Eating - www.thecenternc.org

Thin Within - www.thinwithin.com

To Write Love on Her Arms - www.twloha.com

Truce with Food - www.trucewithfood.com

Wayne Dyer - www.drwaynedyer.com

Wild Soul Movement - www.wildsoulmovement.com

Win the Diet War - www.winthedietwar.com

Books

Books can teach us, take us to another world and help us to learn us some pretty powerful lessons. These books have revolutionized and transformed my life and my way of thinking. I share them here in the hope that they do the same for you!

A Complaint-Free World by Will Bowen
A New Earth by Eckhart Tolle
Almost Anorexic by Jenni Schaefer
The Art of Extreme Self-Care by Cheryl Richardson
Breaking Free from Emotional Eating by Geneen Roth
Conversations with God by Neale Donald Walsche
Do I Look Fat in This? by Jess Weiner
The End of Overeating by David Kessler
Food Guilt No More by Lindsey Smith
Food Mood Girl by Lindsey Smith
The Four Pillars of Awesome Relationships by Marcus Ambrester
Goodbye Ed, Hello Me by Jenni Schaefer
Happiness is a Choice by Barry Neil Kaufman
How to Stop Worrying and Start Living by Dale Carnegie
Integrative Nutrition by Joshua Rosenthal
The Law of Attraction by Jerry and Esther Hicks
Life Doesn't Begin 5 Pounds from Now by Jess Weiner
Life Without Ed by Jenni Schaefer
Life Without Limits by Peter Calhoun
Loving What Is by Byron Katie
Ravenous by Dayna Macy
Shut Up, Stop Whining, and Get a Life by Larry Winget
Soul on Fire by Peter Calhoun

The Slow Down Diet by Marc David
Way of the Peaceful Warrior by Dan Millman
The Way You Do Anything is the Way You Do Everything by Suzanne Evans
We Are Sacred by Tom Lake
Woman Overboard!: Six Ways Women Avoid Conflict and One Way to Live Drama-Free by Rachel Alexandria
Women, Food & God by Geneen Roth

Made in the USA
San Bernardino, CA
21 December 2015